Ellen Gilchrist

Twayne's United States Authors Series

Frank Day, Editor

Clemson University

TUSAS 690

ELLEN GILCHRIST
Pierre G. Walker III

Ellen Gilchrist

Mary A. McCay

Loyola University

Twayne Publishers
An Imprint of Simon & Schuster Macmillan
New York

Prentice Hall International
London • Mexico City • New Delhi • Singapore • Sydney • Toronto

Twayne's United States Authors Series No. 690

Ellen Gilchrist
Mary A. McCay

Twayne Publishers
An Imprint of Simon & Schuster Macmillan
1633 Broadway
New York, NY 10019

Library of Congress Cataloging-in-Publication Data

McCay, Mary A.
    Ellen Gilchrist / Mary A. McCay.
        p. cm. — (Twayne's United States authors series ; TUSAS 690)
    Includes bibliographical references and index.
    ISBN 0-8057-4029-5 (alk. paper)
    1. Gilchrist, Ellen, 1935–   —Criticism and interpretation.
    2. Feminism and literature—Southern States—History—20th century.
    3. Women and literature—Southern States—History—20th century.
    I. Title. II. Series.
PS3557.I34258Z77 1997
813'.54—dc21   97-20635
                                                                            CIP

10 9 8 7 6 5 4 3 2 1

Printed in the United States of America

For
Crispin, Mayo, and Skelly

Contents

Preface

Ellen Gilchrist published her first book in 1979. She was 44 years old and had spent most of her adult life raising her three children. In 1976, at the invitation of the poet James Whitehead, she had entered the University of Arkansas MFA program in creative writing, and although she stayed only a short time and did not finish a degree, her move to Fayetteville and her friendships with the teachers and writers there were important catalysts for her artistic development. Although she dates her professional career as a poet to 1975, a year before she entered the Arkansas program, clearly the move from New Orleans freed her to write and to experiment with fiction as well as poetry.

Several themes emerge from her poetry, short stories, novels, and journals, themes that both connect her with earlier southern women writers and help give her a distinct point of view. Women struggling for a voice and a sense of self, women escaping from confining families and making larger communities for themselves, and women truly coming to understand their place in society and in the world are the women that Gilchrist writes about. Certainly Rhoda Manning, introduced to readers in a story in the collection *In the Land of Dreamy Dreams* in 1981, is one of Gilchrist's most engaging and fully developed characters. She was among the first of her kind for Gilchrist, a young woman who was spunky and gutsy and who questioned why parents loved boys more than girls, why only boys (at least in her family) got to go to the Junior Olympics, and why men always seemed to get to decide how women lived their lives. What was it that diminished girls in the eyes of their parents and in the eyes of the world, she asked, and demanded answers. Although Rhoda succumbed at times to the judgment of family and society, her refusal to define herself within restricting traditions indicates Gilchrist's search for a new way of being a woman in the South.

The publication of her first book of short stories in 1981 by the University of Arkansas Press marked a new beginning for Gilchrist. She became an overnight success with *In the Land of Dreamy Dreams,* and the book was reprinted by Little, Brown in 1985. That publisher has published all but two of her books since. *In the Land of Dreamy Dreams* introduced a new voice to southern fiction. Gilchrist undercut the staid old traditions of New Orleans. The old values and the old money were cast in a very critical light. This book of stories introduced new women who were looking for a life beyond that offered the southern belle. Indeed, Nora Jane Whittington, Gilchrist's most endearing rebel who appears again and again in the short stories, was an antiromantic's romantic, robbing bars to get enough money to follow her true love to California. By 1996, when *The Courts of Love* appeared, Nora Jane had found happiness and fulfillment not with her first true love but with her most enduring. Gilchrist completes Nora Jane's transformation from antiromantic to romantic over a series of several books of short stories, but Nora Jane always surprises and is never conventional.

Gilchrist followed *In the Land of Dreamy Dreams* with a novel, *The Annunciation,* in 1983, which did, indeed, announce that she had command of the longer fiction form. The autobiographical strain that had run through much of Gilchrist's poetry and early fiction became more apparent with this novel. Amanda McCamey, the protagonist, has a good deal in common with Gilchrist herself and with Rhoda Manning, such as obsession with the father figure, conflict with the family, and struggle to define the self outside the spheres normally allowed to southern women. Amanda grew up on a Delta plantation much like the one at which Gilchrist spent her summers as a child; Amanda married young, had a stormy marriage, and then ran off to Arkansas to study. The quest for an articulate self, Gilchrist's own quest, is central to Amanda's experience just as it is to Rhoda's.

In the eighties, Gilchrist seemed to pick up speed and published, in quick succession, *Victory over Japan* (1984) (which won the National Book Award for Fiction), *Drunk with Love* (1986), *The Anna Papers* (1988), and *Light Can Be Both Wave and Particle* (1989). The nineties, too, have been prolific; Gilchrist has published seven books since 1990: *I Cannot Get You Close Enough* (1990); *Net of Jewels* (1992); *Starcarbon* (1994); *Anabasis* (1994); *The Age of Miracles* (1995); *Rhoda, A Life in Stories* (1995); and *The Courts of Love* (1996).

All of Gilchrist's writing focuses on the conflict in women's lives in one form or other. Her characters are trying to escape bad marriages, unhappy love affairs, or terrible families. Wealth does not make Rhoda Manning, Anna Hand, Crystal Weiss, or Amanda McCamey happy, and each woman must look inside herself for some creative force to keep her spiritually alive.

Women's love of men, central to the lives of most of Gilchrist's protagonists, is a constant in southern romantic fiction. The woman, dependent on the man for her livelihood, happiness, and social position, must woo him without seeming to woo and, through marriage, secure

for herself a place in society. For Gilchrist, however, that love is reward-
ing only when it leaves the woman free to be fully herself, and often the
men who would allow that kind of freedom to women are not available.
In Rhoda Manning, Anna Hand, Amanda McCamey, and other female
characters, Gilchrist portrays the struggle to find love and the growing
recognition that, often, the love that is found is destructive. Thus love
lost, unrequited, and unfulfilled becomes another constant in the lives of
Gilchrist's characters.

The city of New Orleans is an artistic touchstone for Gilchrist. Wher-
ever she goes, Nora Jane Whittington will always be, on some level, the
young girl who sold mirlitons from her garden to the best grocery store
in New Orleans, and that grocery store, the famous Langensteins, is
both a physical landmark and a symbolic marker in Gilchrist's uptown
landscape. Other writers whom Ellen Gilchrist knew in New Orleans
have added a dimension to her character and to her writing that enriches
any reading of her books and puts them in a social and historical context. New Orleans, in the mid-seventies, was brimming with poets and
artists, and Gilchrist's pictures of the city and the people have generated
a good deal of conversation about who is who in the fiction. In addition,
the city itself created a perfect cultural backdrop for her characters. New
Orleans, when Gilchrist moved there in the late sixties, was a city in
which time, progress, and political awareness seemed to have stopped.
The Spanish moss hanging from the trees in Audubon Park, the streetcar rattling down Saint Charles Avenue, the large mansions only a street
away from squalid slums—all illustrated the decadent underpinnings of
the society in which her characters lived.

Frank Stanford was certainly the most influential poet in Gilchrist's
life. In fact, he may well have been the most influential person. Intensely brilliant and charismatic, he represented for Gilchrist the possibility of the arts, but more important, he represented a kind of artistic
freedom that she herself was trying to achieve. She met him when she
went to Arkansas in 1976, and he was dead by 1978, but he was instru-
mental in shaping her first book of poems, and he remains alive in many
of Gilchrist's fictional characters. Her constant return to his suicide is
almost a chant about the death of the artist in the late twentieth century. What Stanford's death does for readers, and quite possibly for
Gilchrist, is focus on the need for artists in any society, because a society
without artists is truly dead.

It is possible to trace Gilchrist's emergence as an artist through her
poetry, her journal, her short stories, and her novels. The poetry and jour-

nals, as well as her juvenile story fleshed out in the novel *Anabasis,* offer a skeleton for the development of fully formed characters, and although this grouping is not chronological, it is helpful in understanding how Gilchrist constructs her fiction. Her short stories often follow the growth of characters from childhood into middle age, and by examining all of the collections as a continuum, it is possible to see the way characters change given life experience and circumstances. Finally, her novels look closely at individual growth and at family development, and their textual connections are better seen when they are examined as a group. The chapters have been shaped to emphasize the continuity throughout Gilchrist's oeuvre, not to highlight chronological publication.

Acknowledgments

This book would not have been possible without the help of Douglas McCay, Aimee Cahill, William T. Cotton, Edmund Edmonds, Rose French, Carey Herman, Richard Johnson, Raymond McGowan, Melanie McKay, Richard Mirabelli, T. R. Mooney, Marcus Smith, Sophia Stone, Susan Tucker, and Donna Glee Williams.

I would like to give special thanks to Ralph Adamo, Jason Berry, Rhoda Faust, William Harrison, Don Lee Keith, Ginny Stanford, and Pierre Walker for their cooperation with interviews and research questions.

Chronology

1935   Ellen Gilchrist born 20 February in Vicksburg, Mississippi, the second child and only daughter of Aurora (Alford) and William Garth Gilchrist Jr. Gilchrist spent much of her childhood in Illinois, Indiana, and Kentucky, where her father worked as an engineer. She spent parts of her summers in the Mississippi Delta with her mother's family.

1950   Worked as a columnist for *The Franklin Favorite* in Franklin, Kentucky. Her column was called "Chit and Chat about This and That."

1953   Graduated from Southern Seminary in Buena Vista, Virginia.

1953–1955   Spent her freshman year at Vanderbilt University and her sophomore year at the University of Alabama at Auburn. She also spent a summer session at Emory University.

1955   Married Marshall Peteet Walker.

1956   Son, Marshall Peteet Walker Jr., born 26 July.

1957   Son, Garth Gilchrist Walker, born 10 July.

1958   Divorced Marshall Walker; married for six months to Judge James Nelson Bloodworth.

1959   Remarried Marshall Walker.

1961   Son, Pierre Gautier Walker III, born 29 September.

1963   Divorced Marshall Walker for second and final time.

1967   Graduated from Millsaps College in Mississippi with a B.A. in Philosophy.

1968   Married Frederick Sidney Kullman; moved to New Orleans.

1975   Marked this year as the beginning of her professional poetry career.

1975–1978   Contributing editor for *The Courier,* a New Orleans newspaper, where she worked with Don Lee Keith.

1976   Enrolled in Creative Writing Program at the University of Arkansas, Fayetteville, at the invitation of the poet James Whitehead.

1976–1981   Lived both in Fayetteville and in New Orleans.

1979   *The Land Surveyor's Daughter,* Gilchrist's first book of poetry, published by Lost Roads Press, Fayetteville, Arkansas.

1981   *In the Land of Dreamy Dreams,* Gilchrist's first book of short stories, published by University of Arkansas Press.

1981   Divorced Frederick Sidney Kullman. Permanent residence now Fayetteville, Arkansas.

1983   *The Annunciation,* Gilchrist's first novel, published by Little, Brown and Company (unless otherwise noted, all other books also published by Little, Brown).

1984   *Victory over Japan,* a collection of short stories, published; it won the National Book Award for fiction.

1984   Began broadcasting commentary on the morning edition of National Public Radio. The commentaries were published in *Falling through Space* in 1987.

1985   *In the Land of Dreamy Dreams* republished by Little, Brown.

1985   *Invasions, Incursions, Intrusions, Acts of Love,* a play given two performance stagings in New York. No known copies extant.

1986   *Drunk with Love,* short-story collection, published.

1986   *Riding Out the Tropical Depression,* poetry, published by Faust Publishing.

1988   *The Anna Papers,* novel, published.

1989   *Light Can Be Both Wave and Particle,* short-story collection, published.

1990   *I Cannot Get You Close Enough,* three novellas, published.

1992   *Net of Jewels,* novel, published.

1994   *Starcarbon,* novel, published.

1994   *Anabasis* published by the University of Mississippi
        Press. This novel is based on stories of ancient Greece
        that Gilchrist's mother told her.

1995   *The Age of Miracles,* short-story collection, published.

1995   *Rhoda, A Life in Stories,* short-story collection, pub-
        lished.

1996   *The Courts of Love,* short-story collection, published.

Chapter One
A Portrait of the Artist

Almost any portrait of an artist contains many facets: the precocious child, the emerging artist, the mature craftsperson, and the public figure, to name only a few. As the writer develops, themes often emerge as the focus of many works, tested and fleshed out again and again. Ellen Gilchrist's career as a poet, short-story writer, and novelist reveals several such patterns. Her writing returns repeatedly to themes that place her squarely within a tradition of southern women's writing, but Gilchrist plays out those themes in ways that are specific to her own experience. Further, given her childhood experience outside the South, her writing looks beyond regional borders and asks questions that link her with women writers all over America.

Themes

Gilchrist herself denies that she is a feminist, saying in a most unliberated way, "I like men because they protect me. All my life they have protected me and I believe they will go on doing it as long as I love them in return."[1] However, her books give primacy to women's experience and promote contemporary ways of looking at that experience. The contrast between Gilchrist's stated politics and the freer territory of her imagination produces a freshness of vision that enriches and deepens her fiction. In her books, men do not always protect women but often exploit and damage them. Even women who love men have to find a way to live in the world without their protection because often the men women love are not capable of protecting them. In *Net of Jewels*, Rhoda Manning's husband is abusive, her father controlling, and her lovers much less powerful than she is. In *The Annunciation*, Amanda McCamey's husband wants a Stepford wife, not an intelligent and independent woman. When Amanda chooses a lover, she chooses one young enough to be her child and without money so he cannot control her. Powerful women who make their own choices about life and love emerge from Gilchrist's fiction, and even when they are looking for men to protect them, as Anna Hand of *The Anna Papers* and several short-story collections, often is, they do not give up their sense of themselves as individuals.

Women's emergence is not Gilchrist's only preoccupation; many other motifs run throughout her fiction, as well, such as the relationships between parents and children. Independence from an overwhelming parent or parental figure, most often a charming but dangerously controlling father, is central to the experience of most of Gilchrist's characters, from Rhoda Manning through Anna Hand and countless others who appear only once or twice in short stories and novels. Preoccupation with the father is, for Gilchrist, a focus on origins and power. The daughter's origins should give her power, but instead, the father, in his need to control, weakens the daughter. The issues that arise from the daughter's struggle to free herself from the father while needing the father's love and approval are deeply embedded in Gilchrist's fiction.

Southern families under the influence of such powerful fathers run throughout the catalog of Gilchrist's work. Those families also include powerful women, however, and their role should strengthen the daughters and granddaughters they produce. Unfortunately, that is often not the case. In Gilchrist's first novel, *The Annunciation,* the women of Amanda McCamey's family have outlived their men and therefore should nourish Amanda. Instead the women act as the guardians of tradition and try to form Amanda into a southern belle. Her rebellion, so typical of Gilchrist's young women, represents another common theme in Gilchrist's novels and short stories, the struggle for independence.

Independence, however, is meaningless without love. Gilchrist is a master at portraying the paradox of the independent woman, who struggles to maintain her freedom while becoming more and more a slave to her emotions and a prisoner to the love she feels for a man. Anna Hand, in thrall to her love for the red-haired baby doctor, is a paradigm of the need for love and for security to protect that love. The doctor, unable to leave his wife, cannot offer Anna the sense of being loved totally. Gilchrist, in *Falling through Space,* defines that love when she quotes an ex-Vanderbilt football player who says to her, "Goddammit, you expect us to be gentlemen twenty-four hours a day and ready to kill at a moment's notice" (*FTS,* 153). The writer whose characters struggle so ceaselessly for independence seems, at times, to yearn for a world in which women can escape from responsibility and be happily dependent upon men.

Love and escape go hand in hand for Gilchrist. Escape from the loneliness of the artist is what drives Anna Hand to love. Escape from growing old is what propels Amanda McCamey's need for her young lover, Will. Finally, escape from the tedium and the confinement of an unhappy marriage motivates Rhoda Manning's pursuit of love in extramarital affairs.

On a more philosophical level, Gilchrist looks closely at human behavior in terms of the fall from grace. Her first book, *In the Land of Dreamy Dreams,* whose title is taken from the popular song "Way Down Yonder in New Orleans," opens with a section entitled "There's a Garden of Eden," illustrating her acknowledgment of the imperfections of human life. Her characters are caught up in the struggle to retain their innocence, but winning that struggle depends upon ignoring the world in which they live. Rhoda, Amanda, and Anna, whatever their failings, look squarely at the world and know what it can do to people. Some of Gilchrist's more naive characters think they can escape the consequences of original sin simply because they have money. Gilchrist's first book of short stories certainly undercuts that notion. LaGrande McGruder of the title story in *In the Land of Dreamy Dreams* falls from grace most egregiously. Her only escape from the knowledge of her fall is to throw herself back into the decadent, moneyed society that reared her and "see if anyone she liked to fuck was hanging around the pool."[2] The lives of the rich reverberate with a spiritual bankruptcy that drives Gilchrist's stronger characters in search of something more than money and comfort.

Related to the fall from grace is the ubiquitous romantic quest for innocence. The moments when young women reveal their essential innocence in the face of a corrupt world are important ones for Gilchrist. Nora Jane Whittington, the spunky young woman of several Gilchrist short stories, is an innocent in the world, and her naive search for her lover is a search for the Garden of Eden. In the Nora Jane stories, the search for the right love and the quest for paradise go hand in hand, and in that sense, Nora Jane is perhaps Gilchrist's most romantic character.

Ultimately, many of Gilchrist's themes can be summarized in terms of a quest. Gilchrist's own life has been a quest for identity, wholeness, artistic freedom, and love, and her quests are mirrored in those of her characters, especially her female characters, and most profoundly in her women artist characters. The quest, heroic in its intent and in its processes, grounds Gilchrist's fiction in a romantic tradition that allows her free rein both to create a world in which her characters can flourish and to criticize the real world in which they must survive. Ironically, Gilchrist is also a realist who sees the flaws of the modern South, especially of the decadent city of New Orleans, with a very clear sense of what is wrong with that world.

As her poetry, journals, and fiction develop, Gilchrist more and more illustrates her poetic and fictional themes from a deeply personal past that gives her stories and many of her characters an autobiographical cast. Her experience and that of her characters merge in a world in which Gilchrist can both create her own past and refashion it in a romantic image. Because of that process, much of what happens in her narratives happens to different characters in the same way. For example, in her created worlds, the process of becoming an artist dramatizes Gilchrist's own growth as a writer; her artist characters themselves seem facets of her own personality. Rhoda Manning, Anna Hand, and Amanda McCamey share the struggle to be writers with each other and with their creator, but even more, their histories and experiences overlap in such a way as to make them seem bound to one another through Gilchrist's own history.

Rhoda Manning is most closely related to her creator in terms of her past and her experiences, and Gilchrist herself asserts that, although some of Rhoda's experiences are made up, others are "blatantly autobiographical."[3] It is through Rhoda that readers begin to see the connection between Gilchrist and her characters; it is through Rhoda that readers enter into the life of Ellen Gilchrist.

Childhood

Born in Vicksburg, Mississippi, in February 1935, Gilchrist spent the early years of her life in the midst of an extended southern family. Had World War II not taken her engineer father and his family to the North in the early forties, Gilchrist herself might never have experienced any other life than that of a privileged southern white girl. Even so, she returned with her mother each summer to Hopedale Plantation in Mississippi, where the facts and the fictions of Gilchrist's southern experience merge. *Falling through Space,* a compendium of National Public Radio broadcasts, magazine articles, and memoir-type musings, both idealizes and eulogizes the world of Gilchrist's ancestors and sets the stage for the childhoods of both Rhoda Manning and Amanda McCamey. Gilchrist, while filling her characters' lives with family tensions and conflicts, asserts that her childhood was happy, idyllically happy, and her descriptions of the world she lived in and the family she grew up in often conflict with the unhappiness of her autobiographical protagonists such as Rhoda and Amanda. The unhappiness that Rhoda experiences could perhaps mirror what went on in Gilchrist's life when her father moved north. At that time, Gilchrist lost the close family bonds of Hopedale Plantation and was thrown into a cold northern world. Not only did she lose her large protective family, but her father moved so frequently that Gilchrist could not sink roots anywhere. Her own list of schools attended attests to the many disruptions. She spent her childhood winters in Indiana, Illinois, and Kentucky, attending several different schools, with the longest term being spent in Harrisburg, Illinois. Those years are reflected in the stories of Rhoda Manning's childhood. The war years, the years of moving during which Rhoda unhappily leaves friends, schools, and even her first love are, possibly, reflective of Gilchrist's own childhood feelings about dislocation. Each move was, for Rhoda and perhaps for Gilchrist, like being thrown out of Eden, and that experience is replayed time and again in Gilchrist's fiction. The moves are also indicative of the disruption to Gilchrist's own sense of herself as a writer. One transit was particularly difficult because Gilchrist had secured a job as a columnist for the *Franklin Favorite* in Franklin, Kentucky. At the age of 15, Gilchrist already thought of herself as a writer, and this job validated her sense of herself. Having to give up the excitement and the prestige of having her own column because of her father's job heightened the sense of helplessness that adolescents already feel. In *Net of Jewels,* Gilchrist illustrated, through Rhoda, the impotent rage children often feel at their powerlessness to control their own destinies. Rhoda must move when her father's job demands it; she has no say in the politics of the household. Like chattel, she is moved with the furniture and must accept her new home regardless of her feelings.

Despite the constant uprooting, Gilchrist had a strong sense of belonging to Hopedale and to her extended family there. In *Falling through Space* she recalls that, when she was away from Hopedale, she would write letters to the people there and say, "I will be there as soon as I can. Make some pound cakes and tell everyone I am coming" (*FTS,* 45). That sense of connection is reiterated when Gilchrist writes of family gatherings. Her sense of returning to a place that has family connections enriches her memories of childhood and creates a setting for her fiction. One such instance of the writer's return to her roots is her vivid recall of a family Thanksgiving in 1967. Gilchrist, then divorced from her husband, Marshall Walker, had returned to Millsaps College to finish her degree in philosophy and depended heavily on her parents for help with the care of her three young sons. The Thanksgiving she recalls was celebrated at her parents' home at Summerwood in Rankin County, Mississippi. Gilchrist, her three boys, her brothers, and her six nieces were all at home for the holiday. Gilchrist decided to have a family Olympics to set the record straight on her place in the family. Her motivation was patently close to the motivation Rhoda expresses in the short story "Revenge" for her competitions with her brother, Dudley Manning. Gilchrist's older brother, Dooley, like Rhoda's brother, Dudley, was always both an idol and a thorn in Gilchrist's childhood. When he was a child, he had placed third in a Junior Olympics competition that Gilchrist herself had not been allowed to enter. As an adult, Gilchrist wanted to beat that paragon of a brother. The writer reveals, "I would surprise and conquer my older brother" (FTS, 43) in a race. That was the motivation for Gilchrist's family Olympics, but Dooley refused to cooperate. Throughout Gilchrist's childhood, Dooley either "refused to race. Or else he raced but didn't try and infuriated me by letting me win" (FTS, 43). The adult experience, recounted in Falling through Space, recapitulates and recalls the experience of childhood, and Gilchrist, remembering, is filled with the same feelings of love and hatred she experienced as a girl. Family bonds are tested and strengthened throughout life, and Gilchrist describes her bond with Dooley, a bond that makes it hard for her to deal with her ambivalence about their relationship: "On top of everything else he has done to me he goes on loving me more than I love him, as a Big Brother should. I know, for example, that if I was in a hospital with some terrible cancer and no one else would do it, he would shoot me if I asked him to" (FTS, 152).

Family ties, but also family myths, such as the illusion of Dooley's love, are central to Gilchrist's sense of herself as a storyteller. Her poetry valorizes her father, or the mythical father, and her children. Anna Hand's childhood in North Carolina mimics, in its intense family relationships, the childhood Gilchrist remembers at Hopedale. Finally, the ambivalence that arises from the myths runs like a vein of ore throughout Gilchrist's work. Her characters idealize family relations while attempting to escape from the very families they mythologize.

College

Gilchrist, much like her character Rhoda Manning, had a sketchy college career. In 1953, after graduating from Southern Seminary in Buena

Vista, Virginia, she entered Vanderbilt University. If Gilchrist's portrayal of Rhoda's first year at college is any indication, the writer was excited and challenged by the intellectual life at the university. However, like Rhoda, Gilchrist, too, transferred to the University of Alabama at Auburn and found the experience much less intellectually stimulating. After a summer session at Emory University, Gilchrist eloped with Marshall Walker, and for the next nine years, her formal education ceased. When she divorced Walker for the second and final time in 1963, she continued her education by attending Millsaps College in Mississippi, where she received a B.A. in philosophy in 1967. The 12 years it took her to finish her undergraduate degree were a time of enormous change for Gilchrist, and those changes and Gilchrist's response to them are, again, best chronicled in *Net of Jewels,* published in 1992. In this book, Rhoda Manning's chronology registers some of the important milestones in Gilchrist's own life. There are times in that book in which the autobiographical blurs with the fictional, and very little seems to separate the character and the author.

Marriages

In 1955 Gilchrist quit college and eloped with Marshall Peteet Walker. That first marriage resulted in the birth of two sons, Marshall Peteet Walker Junior in 1955 and Garth Gilchrist Walker in 1956. Within a year of Garth's birth, Gilchrist divorced Walker and married an Alabama judge, James Nelson Bloodworth, a man she was clearly not compatible with. That marriage lasted only six months, and when the divorce was finalized in 1959, Gilchrist remarried Marshall Walker. Her third son, Pierre Gautier Walker III, was born in 1961. The marriages to Walker, although they lasted a total of six years, were not tranquil. Gilchrist found the sudden addition of children into an unstable relationship to be a very taxing experience. Marshall Jr. and Garth were born within a year of each other, and within a year of Garth's birth, Gilchrist had divorced her husband and hastily married a man whose public position gave Gilchrist status but whose personal relationship with her was completely unsuccessful. Between 1955 and 1959, Gilchrist had married three times, had divorced twice, and had two children. During those turbulent years, remembered in *Net of Jewels,* Gilchrist might well have taken the path of escape that Rhoda spoke of: "We were drunk every day. . . . It was how we escaped. We never would have gotten free without it. It was the gate, the open sesame."[4]

Her fourth marriage, to Frederick Sidney Kullman, took place in 1968 when her youngest child, Pierre, was seven years old. At that time, shortly after having finished her studies at Millsaps College, Gilchrist and her sons moved to New Orleans. And those decades in New Orleans appear again and again in her fiction. Although she marks 1975 as the year she began her professional poetry career, all the years she spent in New Orleans were certainly grist for her fiction and for much of her poetry.

New Orleans

If Gilchrist sought escape from too-close parental control in her move to New Orleans, she did not find freedom. Instead she found yet another marriage that proved as tumultuous as her others. Kullman, known as Freddy, was a New Orleans lawyer who acted as a surrogate father to Gilchrist's sons, especially Pierre. In that, he is much like the second husbands of Rhoda Manning and Crystal Manning Weiss (a character who appears in several short stories throughout Gilchrist's collections). Each of those men takes over the care of a son by another man, and each tries to give the child a sense of belonging. King Mallison, Crystal Manning Weiss's son, might well be a composite of Gilchrist's two older boys, Marshall and Garth, although Mallison is older when he becomes the stepson of Manny Weiss. Mallison rebels against his stepfather, gets into drugs, and finds escape from his new family in his friendship with the poet Francis Alter. As indicated by Ginny Stanford, Marshall Walker, Gilchrist's oldest son, had a close relationship with the poet Frank Stanford, and Stanford's death was very disturbing to the young man.[5] Gilchrist's youngest son, Pierre, is richly portrayed as Teddy in the Rhoda stories and as the young girl Crystal Anne in the series of stories about Crystal Manning Weiss.

The Crystal stories are significant because they often feature another important character, Traceleen, who narrates many of the pieces and whose vision of what is going on in Crystal's marriage to Manny Weiss is a significant one both for the characters in the stories and for the reader. In the stories narrated by Traceleen (who is modeled after Gilchrist's own maid, Rosalie Davis, to whom *In the Land of Dreamy Dreams* is dedicated), the maid creates a voice that both condemns the behavior of her employer and gives her a way of escaping the life that is killing her.

Clearly, New Orleans, for all its social advantages and for all of Gilchrist's fascination with that world, took its toll on her personal life.

That cost is evident in all Gilchrist's female characters who reflect some of her New Orleans experiences. Rhoda Manning finds the city emotionally killing and culturally dead; Amanda McCamey is nearly destroyed by drink until her maid, Lavertis, saves her from alcohol and helps her focus her talent and goals sufficiently to escape her marriage and her social set. Crystal Manning Weiss, too, must escape drink and the oppressive world of the New Orleans rich in order to make her life work, and it is her maid Traceleen who makes that escape possible. All the characters who create a composite for Gilchrist to look at her own experience also share the writer's need for a creative outlet and are mentored by a figure much like Gilchrist's own maid. Rosalie is important both in the fiction and in Gilchrist's life because she offered Gilchrist a calm and steady presence in a world that was often close to being overwhelmed by marital, parental, and personal conflicts.

Two stories that focus on the violence of these conflicts are "Miss Crystal's Maid Name Traceleen, She's Talking, She's Telling Everything She Knows," and "The Stucco House." In both stories, the women, Crystal and Rhoda, fall or are pushed down the stairs. In the first story, Traceleen asserts, "Miss Crystal hasn't ever fall down in her life, drunk or sober, or have the smallest kind of an accident."[6] In the later story, Teddy, Rhoda's youngest son, says, when telling his uncle about the accident, "She said Eric [her husband] tried to kill her. She always says things like that when she's hung over."[7] The two tellings of the event indicate that Gilchrist, over time, has changed her attitude toward the women characters in their struggles with their husbands. It is clear in the first story that the narrator believes that Manny Weiss has pushed his wife down the stairs. In the second story it is equally clear that Teddy is dissociating himself from his mother's insistence that his stepfather Eric has pushed her down the stairs. In fact, Teddy goes even further; he asserts, "If she divorces Eric, I'm going to live with him" (*AM*, 122–23). By focusing on Teddy's response to the situation, Gilchrist indicates a change of attitude toward the women who represent her experience. No longer entirely sympathetic with the histrionics, Gilchrist conveys an increasing authorial distance through the eyes of a young boy. Gilchrist is also rewriting her own past. No longer is it fraught with high drama and accusation. Gilchrist, looking back on her marriages, distances herself from the upheaval by examining events through the eyes of a young boy and sees them in a much less self-dramatizing way.

Gilchrist pictures New Orleans as the scene of a marriage trap for many of her characters, but it was also the location of real creative growth for her. She wrote articles for the *Courier,* a New Orleans weekly newspaper edited and published by Philip Carter. She wrote poetry that was sometimes published in the *Courier,* and she made connections with mentoring friends who helped her begin to focus herself as a writer. In the years between her move to New Orleans and her matriculation in the University of Arkansas writing program in 1976, she was slowly developing a sense of herself as a writer. From 1976–1979, Gilchrist was a contributing editor of the *Courier,* and in 1977 she was an associate editor of *Barataria,* a literary magazine edited by Ralph Adamo and Louis Gallo. While she traveled back and forth between writing workshops at the University of Arkansas and social and familial obligations in New Orleans, Gilchrist began to articulate a critique of the narrow, class-conscious world of the city. Her experience as the wife of a prominent lawyer in New Orleans gave her the opportunity to see that world up close. Her personal experiences shaped the experiences of Rhoda Manning, Amanda McCamey, and Crystal Weiss. As those three women suffer through the stultifying social engagements required of their class, they rebel against the closed world of upper-class New Orleans and finally take some tentative steps to free themselves. During the seventies, Gilchrist, too, was charting her own path toward self-sufficiency.

In addition to the social constrictions, other elements of the old southern city are an important part of Gilchrist's fiction. The stately moss-draped live oaks in Audubon Park, the houses on State Street, the French Quarter, and the neighborhood markets and bars all ground Gilchrist's fiction in a time and a place. In fact, although Gilchrist wrote stories set in other places, her New Orleans fiction is always the richest in terms of setting and ambience. The insulation of the city's rich from the harsh realities of life, the slow southern afternoons on the tennis court or at the club, the culture of drinking, and the stringent code of behavior for the southern woman add to the depth of Gilchrist's critique of modern life. In Gilchrist's fictional world, the city has not grown or progressed. It and its wealthy inhabitants exist in a past that died long ago, and the fictions that people subscribe to are in sharp contrast to the lives people live outside the gates of the palatial houses on Saint Charles and State Streets. Gilchrist was certainly aware of the huge gap between the lives of people in her circle and those of her maids. By giving working women like Traceleen and Lavertis voices in her fiction, Gilchrist highlights another, deeper reality about human behavior that many of her characters are unwilling to accept. She understands that her women characters, in order to be fulfilled, must find meaningful relationships with others and must do useful work.

Friendships

Perhaps one of the most important friendships of her time in New Orleans was with Rhoda Faust, the owner of the Maple Street Bookshop, an important meeting place for writers in New Orleans. Gilchrist asked Faust for permission to use her name in her first Rhoda Manning story, and the character burgeoned into life, not to be repressed or forgotten. Faust met Gilchrist through Faust's mother, who started the bookstore, and when Faust began to work there permanently and then took it over in 1970, she came into frequent contact with Gilchrist. In 1979 Faust hosted a book signing at the store for *The Land Surveyor's Daughter,* and when *In the Land of Dreamy Dreams* was published in 1981, Faust read the book with curiosity. Although many of the uptown set were dismayed by how close to the bone Gilchrist cut in her incisive criticism of the uptown New Orleans set, Faust herself was shocked at how perceptive Gilchrist was about the conflicts she had confronted as a young woman native to the city. Gilchrist, she felt, had not only used her name, but actually saw very deeply into her own character, a realization that was actually a bit daunting.[8] Rhoda might be highly autobiographical, but she also represented something in Faust as well, so in a sense, the character Rhoda has two progenitors. In a letter from Fayetteville postmarked 30 September 1981, Gilchrist wrote to Faust, "you are one of my heroines of the spirit,"[9] an accolade that speaks to the deep connection between the two women and to the importance of Faust in Gilchrist's development as an artist. After the success of *In the Land of Dreamy Dreams,* Faust took the opportunity to ask Gilchrist for a short story or a speech to publish. She had started Faust Publishing and had published a few short pieces by Walker Percy. She felt that Gilchrist would be a natural author to publish because of her connection to New Orleans and because of the personal connection between Gilchrist and herself. Gilchrist suggested that Rhoda publish some of the poems that she had been working on since 1975, and the two began to plan the book. They spent an intensive weekend reading through the poems, and Gilchrist gave Faust helpful insights into the poems and their background. Finally, though, the poet let the publisher choose the poems for the volume *Riding Out the Tropical Depression,* which had a regular edition run of 300 copies and a deluxe run of 50.

Another friend, Don Lee Keith, worked with Gilchrist on the *Courier*. Gilchrist's tenure at the paper lasted from 1975 until 1978, when the paper closed. During that time Gilchrist published poetry and a variety of articles on marriage, psychotropic drugs, and Asian immigrants. One of her short stories, which later appeared in *In the Land of Dreamy Dreams* as "The President of the Louisiana Live Oak Society," also served as a cover piece for an issue of the *Courier*.

Keith was a contributing editor at the paper while Gilchrist was there, and he worked closely with her. He had noticed a poem by Gilchrist in the *Courier* and, witnessing her pique at the typos in the poem when the newspaper was published, befriended her. His articles, too, had suffered from the same careless typesetting so he was prepared to sympathize with Gilchrist. The two "giggled a lot" and were "tolerated" in their behavior at the *Courier* and knew that "their conspiratorial attitudes were being tolerated, not encouraged."[10]

In 1975, when Gilchrist joined the *Courier,* Keith had just returned from two years in Virginia, where he had written for the *Washington Post* and *Rolling Stone* while on a National Endowment for the Arts grant. He had lost two manuscripts in a fire and returned to New Orleans damaged by that loss. Gilchrist was, at that point, very uncertain about her future as a writer. "She did not know," Keith observed, "if writing would be a safe country" (DLK Interview), so their friendship developed around their writing and their uncertainties about their craft.

One story that Keith did on a putative kidnapping in New Orleans became the subject of another Gilchrist short story, "Traceleen Turns East," published in *Light Can Be Both Wave and Particle*. Although Gilchrist did not work on the newspaper article, she accompanied Keith when he went to interview the "victim." Neither he nor Gilchrist nor the *Courier* editor, Philip Carter, believed that a kidnapping had occurred, but the incident became grist for Gilchrist's fiction and a way of exploring characters in a humorous situation.

Gilchrist and Keith shared interests in movies, books, New Orleans life, and the arts. In 1977, Gilchrist invited Keith to accompany her to the Mississippi Arts Festival in Jackson. There, Gilchrist met Tennessee Williams, who later said of her that she was "a little like Maggie the cat [in his play *Cat on a Hot Tin Roof*] without claws" (DLK interview). That picture of Gilchrist helps to illustrate both the earthy realism of her fiction as well as the gentleness with which she treats even her most aberrant characters.

New Orleans of the seventies was, for Keith, very different from today's city. It was a world in which writers like Gilchrist could look at their own personal and emotional crises as games. "Not knowing how to solve them [the problems], we just pretended they were another round of pitching horseshoes" (DLK Interview). However, those games became for Gilchrist a way into her fiction. They gave her a point of view and a perspective on her own life that allowed her to gain sufficient ironic distance from the crises and traumas of her characters so she could be both critical and sympathetic.

Another friend, Ginny Stanford, the widow of the poet Frank Stanford, had an important impact on the visual aspects of Gilchrist's books. Gilchrist bought her first paintings from Ginny Stanford; she used Stanford's paintings on the jackets and paperback covers of several of her books, and the two have enjoyed a rich and sustaining friendship. Ginny Stanford's husband, Frank Stanford, was the model for the poet-mentor Francis Alter, who appears in much of Gilchrist's fiction. In a sense, the friendship was a double one; Gilchrist learned from and grew artistically as a result of her friendships with the poet and the painter, and portraits of Ginny Stanford are reflected in Gilchrist's female artist figures throughout her fiction.

Gilchrist became interested in meeting Ginny Stanford as a result of buying two of her paintings. Stanford's husband, Frank, was, as Stanford says, the middleman in the transaction; he arranged for Gilchrist to buy them. Because Gilchrist was studying in Fayetteville and Frank Stanford was spending a lot of time at the university, Gilchrist got to know him and, through him, discovered Ginny Stanford's work. Gilchrist was immediately taken by Stanford's paintings and managed to meet the artist when Gilchrist arranged a show for Stanford at a New Orleans gallery. Ginny Stanford's story of their meeting, recorded in an interview on 1 August 1996, illustrates just how closely Gilchrist's characters followed in their creator's footsteps. Gilchrist, dressed in a black suit and a string of pearls, met Ginny Stanford for the first time at the Moissant Airport in New Orleans. Gilchrist was on her way to the wedding of her maid, Rosalee, and invited Stanford along. After the reception, Gilchrist discovered that she had locked her keys in her Mercedes and none of Rosalee's nephews could break in. Gilchrist had to call her husband to pick the two women up and take them to the opening. Of course, Kullman was none too happy, but Gilchrist was completely at ease; "she just kept talking . . . Sort of a constant stream of dialogue" (GS Interview).

Moments like the one Ginny Stanford experienced fill the pages of Gilchrist's fiction. Stanford, because she was a working artist when Gilchrist was entering her apprenticeship at the University of Arkansas, afforded Gilchrist an important friendship that gave her confidence that she could, indeed, break away from the world she had lived in for so long. Stanford also read Gilchrist's early work, because the writer trusted the artist's judgment and valued her criticism.

The friendship between the two women was bonded with the death of Frank Stanford in June 1978. The poet's suicide brought the two women closer together, and Stanford even moved to New Orleans for a short time. Gilchrist helped the widow through a very difficult time and was herself comforted by the presence of someone who knew what she was going through.

By 1981, Ginny Stanford had decided to leave New Orleans and move to California. The two women have kept in touch over the years; Gilchrist has visited Stanford there and has made use of the landscape of northern California for her more recent Nora Jane stories. Throughout the years, Gilchrist has continued to use the artist's pictures on her book covers.

Arkansas

Perhaps the most important step Gilchrist took to free herself from the cloyingly destructive landscape of New Orleans was to enroll in the Creative Writing Program at the University of Arkansas at Fayetteville. In the mid-seventies, Fayetteville was a small southern town with a special flavor added by the university. Arkansas itself was a bit of a paradox: it had sent J. William Fulbright to the U.S. Senate for several decades, and his liberalism was a hallmark of the sixties and seventies; but Arkansas was the South, and the South has always had a deeply conservative strain. So Fayetteville was, in many ways, a small town with a double identity. It certainly had the ingrained conservatism of the region, but it was also a town dominated by young people with creative ideas and with all the liberal sentiments of the late sixties. Ralph Adamo, who graduated from the University of Arkansas Creative Writing Program a few years before Gilchrist enrolled and who worked with her on several projects in New Orleans, described the city as "a lively university and counter-culture scene. The poets Frank Stanford and C. D. Wright had just started the Lost Roads Press, there were writers and artists working in the town, and it had a distinctly southern version of political and social rebellion."[11]

Fayetteville attracted a world of painters, writers, potters, and other craftspeople with whom Gilchrist cultivated friendships. She met women from the Calabash Pottery Cooperative, a group of five women whose lives and work might well have inspired the portrait of the potter Katie Vee in *The Annunciation*. Gilchrist became more deeply involved with the life of the artistic community when she began to offer financial backing to the Lost Roads Press. Her book *The Land Surveyor's Daughter* was published by the press as the 14th in its series, and although it came out after the death of Frank Stanford, the book still bears the hallmarks of his design for the Lost Roads Press books.

While at the university, Gilchrist worked with William Harrison on short stories and with Jim Whitehead, the poet, whom she considers one of her two best friends.[12] In speaking of her time there, Harrison remembered that Gilchrist entered the poetry workshop but had not, when she first arrived, written any fiction. Although Gilchrist did not stay long at the university, Harrison did encourage her to write fiction and she showed him several drafts of the story that eventually appeared in *In the Land of Dreamy Dreams* as "Rich." Harrison worked with Gilchrist on the story over a period of several months and noted in a letter that "our longest discussion on that first story focused on the last paragraphs; time after time, they just didn't read well. I finally said, 'Look, Ellen, you're a damn poet. Work out the cadences. Especially the name of that dog.' She laughed and kept working until the flow worked very well."[13] That story became the "university entry for the annual INTRO competition and was a winning entry published there" (Harrison Letter).

Harrison remembers that while she was in Fayetteville, Gilchrist really participated in the life of the program. She went to intramural softball games, attended parties, and really seemed to enjoy the give-and-take of student life. Even though she did not stay in the program long, people remembered her and were genuinely pleased when she won the National Book Award for *Victory over Japan* (Harrison Letter).

Perhaps the most significant relationship Gilchrist formed in Arkansas was with the poet Frank Stanford. Of her friendship with him, Ginny Stanford has said, "When Ellen met Frank, she just naturally recognized his expansive brilliance and responded to it by wanting to learn everything about poetry that he could teach her" (GS Interview). So profound and lasting was the impact of Frank Stanford on Gilchrist that she named the poet in her stories after him: she kept Stanford's first name, and she used the last name of Stanford's adoptive mother, Dorothy. Dorothy Alter married A. F. Stanford when the poet was three, hence Frank Stanford, but the poet's original name, Frank Alter, has been kept alive, too, just as the poet's spirit has been kept alive by his several reincarnations in Gilchrist's fiction. He appears as an imposing presence, a talisman, a memory, a fleeting picture, a name dropped throughout Gilchrist's fiction in a way that allows the writer to immortalize the poet. Stanford was, as Ginny Stanford remembers, "brilliant, charismatic, strikingly handsome" (GS Interview), which was a powerful combination in a man both for the writer and for her fictional women. Frank Stanford was not only a mentor to Gilchrist, he was also a myth incorporated into her mythological world.

First Steps

The highly creative atmosphere of the University of Arkansas helped Gilchrist take the final step toward self-fulfillment. Her work in Whitehead's Poetry Workshop resulted in her first book of poems, *The Land Surveyor's Daughter,* and it reveals how much New Orleans—as a place and as an idea—influenced Gilchrist. While she struggled to escape the confining social milieu, she stored up images of the city that vivified her poetry. Frank Stanford died before Gilchrist's book of poetry was published, but he had spent the three weeks prior to his suicide in New Orleans visiting and working with Gilchrist on the book of poems. Adamo even remembers encountering Stanford during that last trip to New Orleans. The poet was writing long discursive letters to his wife, Ginny, and to his mistress and collaborator at the press, C. D. Wright. Adamo was to learn only a few days later that those letters were the poet's will. Stanford left each of the women specific rights to his poetry and fiction. Then he flew home on the morning of 3 June 1978; that evening, he shot himself three times in the chest while at the house he shared with C. D. Wright and the Lost Roads Press. Ginny Stanford, who lived on a farm about 80 miles outside Fayetteville, was also in the house at the time, and so the wife and the mistress were present when the poet committed suicide (RA Interview).

In her story "Among the Mourners" in *The Age of Miracles,* Gilchrist draws a riveting parallel to the chaos, anger, and grief experienced by members of the artistic communities in Fayetteville and New Orleans over Frank Stanford's death; that story also acts as a sort of wake for the poet. Adamo recalls that James Whitehead opened his house for people to stay and talk about Stanford; the three-day wake was an orgy of grief (RA Interview). Gilchrist remembers and reconstructs the wake in her short story; that the story is told from the point of view of the daughter of the house, a person who does not fully understand the implications of adult grief and uncertainty, adds an ironically chilling dimension to the tale.

Free at Last

If the writing program at the University of Arkansas at Fayetteville helped Gilchrist to find a voice and a genre to express her sense of who she was as an artist, the locale appealed to her for other reasons. It was off the beaten southern belle track. In Fayetteville, she was not expected to behave as the wife of an important lawyer. Further, she would not have to live up to the expectations of the New Orleans wealthy. She could be seen as herself, not an extension of her husband or her children. Finally, Arkansas was also a mecca for artists of all kinds, and Gilchrist found many of them helpful mentors, good friends, and charming conversationalists. However, she felt she had to publish her first book of fiction before she could be really free.

That book, *In the Land of Dreamy Dreams,* was published in 1981 by the University of Arkansas Press because Gilchrist was too uncertain of her voice to send her manuscript to the commercial presses. The book depended heavily on New Orleans, the city she was trying to escape, as both a mythic city and a kind of hell for the writer. Gilchrist's images of rich, unhappy women spoke to people beyond the city and beyond the South, and the book was a popular and critical success. Gilchrist had found her voice.

The reception of *In the Land of Dreamy Dreams* freed Gilchrist from her psychological dependency on New Orleans; in effect, she had exorcised the ghost of the rich southern belle. She had gone to Arkansas to become a writer, and she had succeeded. The next steps were legal freedom from her marriage to Kullman and a permanent move to Fayetteville. These she accomplished, also in 1981, when she bought a house and moved. She claimed that she moved because she could live cheaply in Arkansas and devote all her time to writing, but the move also signaled her declaration of independence. She, like Amanda McCamey, would live alone, write, and be truly free.

The Public Figure

After the publication of her first novel, *The Annunciation,* in 1983, Gilchrist became a public figure; she was "the writer." Her characters spoke to the struggles of young women all over America, and Gilchrist became a popular success. Between 1984 and 1996, Little, Brown and Company published 13 of Gilchrist's books. One of those books was a reprint of her first collection of short stories, and another was a collection of her National Public Radio pieces, but all the rest were new novels and collections of short stories, an enormous output of 12 new books in 12 years. In addition, the University of Mississippi Press published the novel *Anabasis,* which Gilchrist based on classical myths and stories she heard from her mother and wrote as a child.

The Future

Gilchrist continues to let her characters speak for themselves even as they reflect many of Gilchrist's own experiences. Except for Anna Hand, whose death silenced a voice but did not end her influence, Gilchrist's characters seem to have lives offstage, and they constantly press Gilchrist to be heard. Nora Jane Whittington, seen in *Light Can Be Both Wave and Particle* giving birth to twin girls in Freddy Harwood's mountain cabin, resurfaces in *The Courts of Love.* She is 10 years older and her twins are now old enough to have specific characters. The next generation in the writer's family tree is beginning to emerge.

Gilchrist has managed, in all her best fiction, to capture a rare balance between stylistic control and unmediated experience. Her characters say and do what they want; Gilchrist is right when she says they have lives of their own (Gilchrist Interview). They grow and flourish, and readers actually suspect that the characters are home reading quantum physics or out changing the world even when their author isn't writing about them. Gilchrist has also been able to maintain the humor that was so important to her early stories. Although her characters speak their own minds, they do not escape the ironic comment from their creator.

Gilchrist's journey—her quest to find her voice and her struggle to free herself from the confines of a very limiting world—has not ended. Despite her ambivalent attitude toward feminism, her novels and short stories chronicle the journey of each of her women characters to find a self that is not determined or limited by social rules, constricting marriages, or others' definitions. Gilchrist's books also reveal a world that is at once enchanting and very dangerous. Her ability to meld the grotesque and the inane is what prompted Miller Williams, her first editor at the University of Arkansas Press, to refer to her stories as a cross between Flannery O'Connor and Dorothy Parker.[14] At their best they convey a scintillating surface that hides, in many cases, a very disturbing depth. The temptation to be taken care of, the easy slide into the dependency of marriage, and the hunger to be loved at any cost are all obstacles to true freedom; they are also obstacles to emotional growth. Gilchrist's characters, seeking wholeness, often mistake the tangled web of relationships for fulfillment. Gilchrist has never forgotten that conflict in women's lives, and each new work chronicles it more fully. Certainly Nora Jane Whittington's twins of separate fathers are an emblem of that double pull. Tammili is the independent intellectual who looks like her father, Freddy Harwood. Lydia, on the other hand, is more given to the romantic notions her mother had about her father, Sandy George Wade. The two girls together illustrate not just the conflict between the intellect and the emotions, the scintillating surface and the disturbing depth, they make a complete and complex character.

Gilchrist may have already become the servant to her characters, destined to give them voice when they beat down the door of her writing room. Indeed, as Gilchrist's life changes, so do the issues that are important for her characters. In *The Courts of Love*, Nora Jane Whittington looks back dreamily on the struggles of her childhood and her first love, but she also looks forward to a world in which her twins, grounded in the love of their family and strong in their own sense of self, will find independence.

Chapter Two
Poetry, Journals, and Myth

Ellen Gilchrist's reputation is based on her success as a novelist and short-story writer. Viewing her through the lens of her popular fiction, many readers forget that she is also a poet. Gilchrist herself asserted in an interview with Kay Bonetti for the American Audio Prose Library, "I have been all my life a poet and a philosopher. . . . I view life as a wild burgeoning process which I find good."[1] All her work mixes time and space in a new dimension and creates a new world of the imagination. Her two books of poetry, her journals collected in *Falling through Space,* and her historical novel *Anabasis* evidence Gilchrist's enthusiasm for life, uncontrolled and unmediated by stultifying conventions. The two ideas, of being a poet and of finding life "a wild burgeoning process," inform everything Gilchrist writes. Her short stories and novels dramatize the chaos and possibility of life. Her sense of the past, consonant with that of another southerner, is the epigraph for the text of her first book of poems, *The Land Surveyor's Daughter:* "The past is not dead, it is not even past,"[2] William Faulkner asserts; Gilchrist's writing looks into that past and brings it vividly into the present. The works discussed in this chapter help to focus Gilchrist's persistent themes of love, independence, self-fulfillment, and parental conflict and to give voice to those themes. The works also act as a gloss for the writer's more mature fiction that looks beyond romantic love to familial and communal security, and in that, the importance of these works to her thematic message is significant. They form the thematic underpinnings for many other texts.

The past—both the recent history that Gilchrist experienced and the deep past of myth—frames the poetry and journals. The disturbing tensions created by the deeply patriarchal system from which Gilchrist sprang, her own ambivalence about love and freedom, and finally, her need to create the adventurous young woman who escapes the world from which she comes are at the heart of Gilchrist's creative world. As these tensions develop, they deepen and enrich Gilchrist's work.

Poetry

The Land Surveyor's Daughter

The poetic vein that runs through everything Gilchrist writes focuses and crystallizes in *The Land Surveyor's Daughter,* her first book of poetry. Published in 1979 by Lost Roads Press in Fayetteville, Arkansas, the book presented a poetic voice that reached back into the past to understand the present. It is a book of men and women in love, of love lost and betrayed, of the tyranny of men and the resources of women in living under that tyranny, of fathers and children, most specifically fathers and daughters, and finally, it is a book about setting forth and becoming free. It is, in inchoate form, a catalog of all Gilchrist's themes.

Although they lack the satiric momentum of many of Gilchrist's stories, the early poems examine the world that people have made and inhabited for centuries and link cultural ancestors to the present day. The past lives in the present and animates desire and longing; "Passion," the opening poem, introduces the Kha Khan, a mythical figure, as a metaphor to illustrate the power of the past. Just as the Khan, centuries ago, "obliterated whole cities / or diverted rivers from their courses" (*LSD,* 13), so too does he come again in the guise of a lover, "leaning back in the wild grass" (*LSD,* 14). This poem connects not only past and present, but also love and war, a connection that many of Gilchrist's fictional characters illustrate. The book also examines emotions and gives them concrete expression in the lives of characters. In another poem in the volume, a young Pueblo girl trapped in the second year of a drought in A.D. 1276—as many of Gilchrist's modern girls are trapped in the desert of emotional longing—dreams of rivers, of filled water jugs, and of God (or her lover) and prays: "Let your shadow fall to the north / We will find green mesas / We will flow in the days like rivers / We will sing in the nights like trees" (*LSD,* 17). These two poems, "Passion" and "1276 A.D.," reaching far back in time, illustrate Gilchrist's need to establish a continuity between the experiences of her world and those of the past.

The world of women is also central to the first book of poetry. Three poems, collected under the heading "Three Ladies Enter the Seventh Decade," attempt to cover the history of women's suffering and courage and could, perhaps, be said to illuminate the longing of the Pueblo girl. The poems certainly presage the Pueblo girl's life to come should she live to marry and bear children. Septuagenarian women in 1803, 1903, and 1973 recapitulate the rituals of women the world over (childbirth, loss of beauty through aging, etc.) and give a glimpse into Gilchrist's rich stories of the past that later inform her fiction. The first poem in the series is about a woman, Yang Tai-Po, in early nineteenth-century China. She muses about herself: "all day wearing blue silk, / smoking raw black opium, watching / my fingernails turn into antlers, / my feet roll up like pine cones" (*LSD*, 19). Trapped in the palace, she is the mother of princes, but her only command is to "summon the children," her only task, to watch "the sun change places with the moon" (*LSD*, 19). She could just as easily have been one of the bored New Orleans housewives who populate Gilchrist's later fiction. Her own body is not at her service. Her feet have been bound to make her pleasing, just as the young girl who comes to stand beside her will have her feet bound and will be fixed by others' desire.

"Ellen Finnell Taylor Martin," the second poem, is about a woman who later figures as a model for Amanda McCamey's grandmother in Gilchrist's first novel, *The Annunciation*. She has had three husbands: a hunter, a soldier, and a carpenter. The last "made my bed of walnut, then carved / my heart from me" (*LSD*, 19). Gilchrist herself was named after her maternal great-great-grandmother, Ellen Connell Biggs Martin, and Gilchrist imagines in her ancestor the terrible longing of a woman who outlived her husbands but was certainly under their control while they lived. Strong as she is, what the woman in the poem remembers, because all these men have damaged her, are "the cruel hands" of the first husband, "the thin mouth" of the second, and the terrible hurt the third left her with. Maybe the third husband was the one she loved, but she did not give him her heart; he "carved it from" her. She has kept herself whole by outliving the men who would dominate her. Her strength is in her ability to endure.

Mrs. Cole-McCall, the woman of the third poem, seems to have escaped the harsh life and the abiding bitterness of the other two septuagenarians, but she has done so at the expense of her inner life. She is much like the fashionable, empty women who eventually people Ellen Gilchrist's New Orleans. Her type sits at the country club and talks about Jews; she always dresses in the appropriate fashion, and she never stops to think about the passage of time or even her own death. "Life lasts forever" (*LSD*, 20), Mrs. Cole-McCall proclaims as she hurries to be on time for a dress fitting. She must, she reminds herself, have the gardener plant anemones, "so we'll notice when it's spring" (*LSD*, 20). Certainly, Mrs. Cole-McCall is, of the three women, the one who is least aware of the constraints on her life. The three women—one resigned to her deformities, one bitter but resilient, one vacuous—have lived their lives by the standards imposed on them by others. They hint at the struggles of women to come in Gilchrist's fiction.

Fathers, too—the curse and blessing of daughters, the husbands of women who bear their children, the sons of other fathers—are central to Gilchrist's first book of poems, and the title is at least a passing reference to her own father. In the novel *Net of Jewels,* Gilchrist characterizes the father with money and a mighty will that molds his children to his image; in "The Land Surveyor's Daughter," the title poem, he is not fleshed out, but his image looms over the pages of this book as the father's does in *Net of Jewels,* even though the father in the poem has lost the physical attributes of power and "his hips were dried up / like a cow pond in a summer drought" (*LSD,* 26). Just the idea of the father is powerful enough for the daughter in the poem.

The conflict between love and betrayal, central to much southern literature and certainly a core theme for Gilchrist, works its way through the title poem. The father, honorable, optimistic, and brave, counsels: "hold your head up . . . finish anything you start . . . stick with the same job so your boss sees you are loyal" (*LSD,* 26). All the virtues of perseverance, duty, and honor are contained in his advice. The daughter betrays him with her independence and, of course, her own set of values, but he too betrays his past and himself. He is "holed up on the coast . . . spying on a hippie" (*LSD,* 26). The father and daughter have reached the same pass. They are eating the wrong foods, and the father is growing old. How can he hold his head up like he counseled his daughter to do? The circle of time brings the rebellious daughter and the aging father closer and closer together, and the poem indicates that it is possible for love to replace anger.

The father has also left his daughter the legacy of Bacchus. "He poured my first wine" (*LSD,* 29), claims the poet, and that act has given the daughter license. Now, she claims, "I drink with anyone. . . . They come and they go, they take / what they need" (*LSD,* 29). The father both binds the daughter to him and gives her to other men, but she has no freedom when "they take / what they need," leaving her with only telephone "numbers to call" (*LSD,* 29).

All the poems about the father in Gilchrist's poetry swirl around the awful need for love and the terrible loneliness of being a separate person. The daughter must free herself, but that act seems like an act of betrayal, and she punishes herself for her failure to live up to the image the father wanted. "How I betrayed him" (*LSD*, 26), she laments. As Rhoda Manning says in the preface to *Net of Jewels*, "I was cathected by a narcissist" (*NJ*, 3), and that same psychological profile runs through *The Land Surveyor's Daughter*. The daughter, in order to understand and free herself, has to "break the bonds [he] tied [her] with" (*NJ*, 3). In a poem in Gilchrist's second collection, *Riding Out the Tropical Depression*, Gilchrist does finally "create a new father,"[3] and thus frees herself from the awful burden of doing his will. However, she still carries him all her life in her genes, in her children, and into future romantic hungers.

The need for a father's love takes on a new dimension in other poems in *The Land Surveyor's Daughter*. These, written as if to a lover, also focus the poet's quest for love and understanding. The poem "Max, I'm on a DC-10 Writing about Your Winter Pasture at Midnight" echoes with the lament of love going cold, and the speaker demands, "Give me your jacket / Whatever winter offers I will take" (*LSD*, 23). Can a love chilled by loneliness and the daily occasions of life be warmed by desire? On an airplane, the poet sees, etched in the dark past of her memory, her lover's arms, the distant cabin, and the white shadows. A later poem proclaims, "Shut Up, I'm Going to Sing You a Love Song," and that poem features a coming together at the end where "there is nothing to fear" (*LSD*, 39).

In this work, as in most of Gilchrist's work, the question about love looms large, and characters often query how long it can last. Some of Gilchrist's love poems insist that waning love can be recaptured, retrieved before it is totally gone, but often her poems contain only loneliness, the sense that some things cannot be saved. In "Song of the Lonely Streetcar Rider," loneliness is a kind of death, like the death of a "four week foetus / riding out to sea inside the several crabs / which share the spoils of confused paternity" (*LSD*, 41). Yet, even in the moments when the rider is most alone, the streetcar "swings along / picking up passengers at every stop" (*LSD*, 41). Finally the poem states, "No one is alone forever" (*LSD*, 42), a mantra that Gilchrist's characters chant to themselves throughout decades of poems and stories in a kind of desperate hope that they can make it true.

A humorous poem, "The Children of Divorce," solidifies the anger at betrayal and lost love while making amusing observations about human nature. The poem honors the capacity to survive, to turn a bad situation into an advantage, and to bring the past and the present together by use of a series of hotel chits that the children sign "with their old father's / name and their real father's name and the poor bastard / who is going to be their new father's name" (*LSD,* 34). In this poem, which is placed in the book facing a poem for "The Children of Cheramie Cemetery Terrebonne, Parish, Louisiana," the children of divorce are seen as survivors, whereas the children of Cheramie Cemetery are the casualties of life and of love. As the dead children lie in their eternal sleep, nothing can disturb the peace they have found, but they have not experienced life. They died too young and will never have the chance to learn from experience: "Even rain does not enter / La Societe Des Enfantes du Silence" (*LSD,* 35). In these two poems about children, loss is central and survival is never certain. The children of divorce seem resilient and tough; they insist on themselves and on their own survival, but they cannot forget their fathers. The children will be forever bound to the past by loss and betrayal, love and remembering. The dead children are to be mourned because they never had the chance to experience life, love, and struggle, but the living are also casualties.

In "Audio for a Video Tape to Be Played at the Reading of My Will," the poet tells a story that, in its implication and in its setting, prepares for a character who appears in *The Annunciation* as Will, the surveyor, Amanda McCamey's lover. The poem records a story very much like one he tells in that novel. In fact, Gilchrist uses the same story twice: once in the poem and again in the novel. The surveyor has laid out a cemetery for an old woman, a war widow perhaps—"she wears a pair / of Air Corps wings pinned to her shirtwaist" (*LSD,* 36)—and she is unhappy with her cemetery. She wanted the graves to run "east and west lined up with the sun" (*LSD,* 35). The graves don't, and the woman is disappointed and angry and refuses to pay for the job. Her anger at having her wishes thwarted is a reflection of her anger at having no power in life.

Riding Out the Tropical Depression

All the poems in *The Land Surveyor's Daughter* resonate in later stories, but they also create a coherent focus on the father, the past, and the efforts of children to come to terms with both. In that respect, they are a thematic complement to the second book of poems Gilchrist published, in 1986. *Riding Out the Tropic Depression,* published by Faust Publishing, is a group of selected poems written between 1975 and 1985. As Gilchrist says in her introductory note, the poems are printed in the order in which they were written. She also points out that "readers of my fiction will see the inception of ideas and themes that later became

stories or characters. Things that were dark in the poems often turned
into comedies as the work and the mind of the writer became clearer
and more in balance" (*RO,* ix). The dedication of the book, "For my
father, William Garth Gilchrist, Junior, of Jackson, Mississippi, the
finest man I have ever known" (*RO,* xii), highlights again one of
Gilchrist's central themes: the daughter's relationship with the father.
Here it is bound in love but also in seeming deference or submission, for
Gilchrist also writes, "If there are any words he doesn't like he can mark
them out as usual" (*RO,* xii). In this dedication her submission seems
freely given, but in Gilchrist's fiction, submission to the father is more
often a cause of enormous tension and conflict. This dedication, then, is
at best ambivalent, with a note of sarcasm or at least of unresolved
anger.

The first poem in the book, "Marshall," which Gilchrist wrote while
on a vacation in the Caicos Islands, was also "the first piece of writing
[she] had done in seven years" (*RO,* xii). That poem opened up a creative
vein that fed the rest of the book of poems and led to many of her stories. The first poem also contains the line "drunk with love" (*RO,* 1),
which became the title of her third collection of short stories, also published in 1986. There is a resonance between the poems and Gilchrist's
stories, as she herself has asserted, and there is a sense that the poems
were the skeletons for longer prose pieces. It is that skeletal structure
that gives even her most humorous stories an edge of darkness.

The poems in this second collection, while posturing about freedom
and escape, love without responsibility, and a truly idyllic life, are
fraught with darker subtexts. The first two poems to her sons, "Marshall" and "Southpaw," extol her children's power to enchant her, but
also recognize the children's fragility and the poet's uncertainty about
how to love them. She begs, "forgive me / my strange motherhood,
keeper of my eyes and hair" (*RO,* 1). In the fragile vessels of her sons is
the poet's own immortality; the link will, perhaps, help them to
"redeem each other" (*RO,* 1).

The second poem, "Southpaw," portrays Gilchrist's son: "Wearer of
my hair, / keeper of my smile, sixteen years / since your left hand lay
clenched inside / my womb sharing my cigarettes and sherry" (*RO,* 2).
The poet recognizes how easily the very intricate mechanism of the body
can be destroyed and prays that the son, undergoing hand surgery, will
be whole: "God of the opposable thumb, / guide the hands that stitch /
my child's split hand, / that it may grasp its limbs and pull, / may hold,
touch, stroke, love" (*RO,* 2). The terrible burden of mother-love echoes

in that prayer. Whereas one of her earlier poems proclaims that "life is no gift" (*LSD,* 41), the children of *Riding Out the Tropical Depression* are seen as treasures, and those gifts may be withdrawn at any point by fate or the carelessness of a surgeon. The mother is a hostage to the love she bears her sons, and the fear at the center of her love is palpable.

Another poem to a 16-year-old son is lighter in tone, but contains the wreck of lost relationships. In "The Mother of the Sixteen Year Old Disco Fiend," the mother "Can't find her blue silk Dian Von Furstenburg / blouse with the balloon sleeves, can't find her real / suede vest, her liquid silver bracelet, / her lucky planter's hat" (*RO,* 3). The child has appropriated everything. He has taken the mother's possessions, possibly because he cannot possess the mother. He even takes "the gold strap from the alligator opera glasses / his stepfather sent from Nieman's / when he married his other wife" (*RO,* 3). Clothed in the finery of a mother who is not available and a surrogate father who has deserted and betrayed his son, the child arms himself with the "1200 watt blow dryer" and uses the no-longer-appropriately-monogrammed towel to dry his Jeep. Love, need, loss, and betrayal lurk about the edges of the poem in the catalog of articles that the son appropriates from the mother.

In the title poem, "Riding Out the Tropical Depression," the dialogue between lovers escaping from the responsibilities of their lives echoes with the desire for paradise and the firmly grounded knowledge, at least in the woman, that "we fell from grace" (*RO,* 4) and can never recapture Eden. As the man argues that "we'll start anew" (*RO,* 5), the woman counters with reality. She has been through this scene too many times and knows that she and her lover cannot deny or forget the past. We cannot, she asserts, "erase the mothers, / fathers, children, / trust funds, / lovers" (*RO,* 4). Loving as intensely as the man desires involves a loss of self that the woman cannot countenance. She insists, "unsew me now or I will sue" (*RO,* 5). She wants to be freed from her desire. Unromantic about her prospects for perfect love, she finally admits, "P.S., I love you anyway," even though she has just begged, "Oh, let me go away" (*RO,* 6). The conflict between love and freedom is central to much of Gilchrist's fiction, and in the poem the conflict is not resolved. The woman loves no less, but she knows that love will deny her the freedom to be herself.

Two other poems in the volume, "Desire" and "The Chartered Boat," depict the intensity of the conflict between romantic notions of love and the reality that people must live in. In the first poem, the woman sees an ideal man three times in three parts of the world. Once she saw him in "an American / drug store in Paris," once "during intermission / of a ballet in Houston," and "once in Sun Valley / leaning against his poles by a stalled chairlift" (RO, 9). The man is a possible lover, one the woman can dream of but can never possess. She imagines "his long face, / his dark hair leaning into the rain" (RO, 9). She sees "banker's hands" (RO, 9) and knows he is destined to be viewed only from afar. The longing, the knowledge of separateness, and the sense of loneliness that follow are the dark core of Ellen Gilchrist's perspective on romantic love. Her women long for connection, but the mature characters see the idealized lover as unattainable because attainment brings discovery of his flaws. The man in the poem is complete in his own life, his family, his children. This image of the man, precisely because he is unattainable, could well be the prototype for the redheaded baby doctor in much of Gilchrist's -fiction.

"The Chartered Boat" depicts one of Gilchrist's "awesomely spoiled white women" (Bonetti Interview) who runs off with a charter boat captain. The dream of escape, the rejection of responsibility for love, and finally, the awful loneliness of the human condition find expression in the piece. In this poem, the roles of the man and the woman are reversed from the roles in "Riding Out the Tropical Depression." It is the man who feels responsibility and who knows what life really is while the woman dances all night and feeds the naval charts, the maps that tell them where they are, to a goat. Like Crystal Manning Weiss of several Gilchrist stories, the woman has "a rich brother in Africa / connections on the coast" (RO, 12), but she is not grounded in love or commitment.

Two companion poems, "There Will Be Seven Fat Years" and "Where Deer Creek Runs Through Cary," are reminiscences of childhood in the Delta, and they resonate with the pull of the past. Eloquently, Gilchrist remembers a childhood friend and the long days of summer in the Delta when she sold snuff at the country store and put her nickel in the slot machine. The names in the poems are straight out of her childhood—Pierce Nolan, Baby Doll, Ditty, and her cousin Charlie. It is these people who become the characters in her fiction, sometimes keeping their own names, as does Baby Doll—the family maid—who waits on other Gilchrist characters. Gilchrist has claimed in other writings and in interviews that her childhood was happy, and the two poems do capture that sense of contentment with her past. Also, the poems seem to imply that in the happiness of the past is the possibility of happiness in the future, as when "a river of nickels came pouring out" of the slot machine (RO,

16). Balanced against that happiness, however, is the recognition of the havoc the past has wrought on the present, and her fictional heroines, Rhoda Manning and Anna Hand, as well as several of her minor characters, struggle with their destructive pasts in the hope of finding happiness in the present.

In "The New Father," the poet creates, out of her imagination and her need, a new father, one who will say "yes, how good to see you / to be the future through you" (*RO*, 17). This poem implies an unhappy childhood for the poet and, in doing so, undercuts the emotions of the previous poems. No longer censorious, the new father loves his daughter and loves the children she creates to allow him to live in the future. Past and present connect in the future of her children, his grandchildren. The idealized father lives in a paradise, shared by the daughter, in which there is no "dream that is not good" (*RO*, 17). A contrast to the controlling and demanding fathers in most of Gilchrist's fiction, the created father loves unconditionally and accepts uncritically. Indeed, he is a dream.

Much of Gilchrist's primary poetic impulse and her philosophical focus are revealed in the last poem in the book, "There's Some Stuff That Is Always Poetry." The belief that past and present combine in new ways to make the future is central to Gilchrist's philosophy. In this poem, especially, she has clearly articulated the idea that all life is connected, the belief that all life springs from the "slime" and returns to the "muck," and the hope that the word, the poem, will crystallize memory so that we can live beyond death. "Mourn for it all and love it" (*RO*, 19), Gilchrist challenges. This poem, both a realization of the limitations of material existence and an insistence on the possibility of something more, is the spur that goads the writer to continue. It is the word, and "the word was made god" (*RO*, 19).

Both *The Land Surveyor's Daughter* and *Riding Out the Tropical Depression* recognize and celebrate not just the art of poetry but poet friends as well. The story of the life and death of Frank Stanford, the poet who committed suicide in 1978, runs like a leitmotiv throughout Gilchrist's novels and short stories. Even in death, he continues to act as a muse for the writer; he was a true friend. His influence and his talent are celebrated in "The Carnival of the Stone Children" in *The Land Surveyor's Daughter,* and he, along with another New Orleans poet, Ralph Adamo, are her cocelebrants at Mardi Gras in the poem, "The Secretary Who Loved Rex": "Frank holds her / over his head like a flower and the king is charmed" (*RO*, 7).

Gilchrist's poems are acts of memory, creation, longing, love. They are also therapy, a way of understanding, challenging, and recreating the past. The poems in her two collections focus on human need in the material world of her family and friends, on the experiences of her past and her hopes for the future, and on her realization of how language can solidify desire and assuage loneliness. In articulating her own experience and broadening it to try to make it the world's, Gilchrist sets up paradigms that serve her well in her short stories and novels.

Journals

Falling through Space

Gilchrist's book of journals, *Falling through Space,* published in 1987, also serves to help gloss the fiction. Although she refers to them as journals, the book is actually a collection of many of her National Public Radio commentaries, some magazine articles, and other writings. All articulate a number of Gilchrist's themes in an openly personal way. These essays help the reader understand the connections between how Gilchrist views life and how she creates character, setting, and conflict in her novels and short stories.

Divided into three sections entitled "Origins," "Influences," and "Work," and with an index entitled "Provenance," *Falling through Space* is a journey, "a quest for truth, the only journey I [Gilchrist] am interested in going on" (*FTS,* 25). That journey takes Gilchrist back into her past, to the Hopedale Plantation, home of her great-great-grandmother, Ellen Connell Biggs Martin, for whom Gilchrist herself is named. The first section of the journals, while decrying "the boring little domestic details of [her grandmother's] life" (*FTS,* 33), gives a clear glimpse into the process of remembering, loving, and forgiving. It is that process in her "Origins" section that lays the groundwork for, and answers some of the questions about, her fiction. Many of the moments that appear in her fiction are also represented in "Origins," and those incidents grow from the nurturing atmosphere of Hopedale Plantation. Her journals and commentaries reveal the autobiographical vein that runs through her work, but they also show how experience is transmuted into fiction. For example, in an entry that was aired on National Public Radio on 13 January 1985, Gilchrist confesses that she writes for therapy and that one of her novels, *The Annunciation,* was written while her second child was in Alaska working on the pipeline. Gilchrist was completely out of touch with her child but could not stop mothering. She says, "It's pitiful. It drives you crazy. It drives you to write novels about adoption" (*FTS*, 34). The connection in her mind is the lost child, a loss that *The Annunciation*'s Amanda McCamey suffered most of her life. Later, in a story in her collection *Light Can Be Both Wave and Particle*, Gilchrist gives Amanda back her child, grown, with a child of her own.

"Origins" also brings Gilchrist's writing life full circle. The last selection in that section, "Knowing Gaia," celebrates the happy childhood, the sights, smells, and memories of a happy early life that was nonetheless overshadowed by war. That war is the darkness beyond the protective wall of happiness that families construct. Gilchrist and her family must venture outside the wall because her father must travel, building military installations and airfields. Once outside the wall, the young child is not so safe in the world, and Gilchrist's letters and her diary entry, written toward the end of the war, indicate the price paid for leaving home. Her older brother Dooley lost an eye, just as the character Rhoda Manning's brother, Dudley, did, and "there is a gold star on the door across the street" (*FTS*, 47), indicating a war death. No one is safe; nothing is permanent.

The second section of *Falling through Space* is also a mixture of National Public Radio pieces and articles written for magazines. Whereas the first section focuses on childhood memories and family connections, the second examines influences that affected Gilchrist's writing. Her extensive reading in science, philosophy, and poetry, her search for a way to speak of experience, and her quest for a means of making connections with her readers are the main subjects of this section.

One of the most profound influences on Gilchrist, as illustrated in a brief piece entitled "My Fiftieth Year to Heaven," was the Mississippi artist Walter Inglis Anderson. For Gilchrist, Anderson's life and work are a model for the artist, visual or verbal. A man of genius, Anderson worked among his family in a small community in Ocean Springs, Mississippi. "No one bothered him. No one told him to stop, or to do it another way. So he just got up every morning and did the work of a genius" (*FTS*, 67). His life represents for Gilchrist the freedom of the artist—"Genius is like a wild thumbprint" (*FTS*, 67)—and Anderson's genius speaks to Gilchrist both in his paintings and in his writing. "True art consists of spreading wide the intervals so that the imagination may fill the spaces between the trees" (*FTS*, 67), Anderson counseled, and many of Gilchrist's artist figures—Amanda McCamey, Anna Hand, Rhoda Manning, and Lydia Manning, the painter—accept the need to allow the imagination free rein. They also accept another Anderson principle, "The normal or even fairly normal man has to be almost knocked down physically to be anything but sublime" (*FTS*, 68), and they intuitively understand their own sublimity—their largeness of character. The characters also realize that their quest to achieve that sublimity is the subject of much of their life and work. They all question, with Anderson, "What reason is there against man realizing his sublimity" (*FTS*, 68), and none knows the answer. All, however, seek to help those they love—their families, their children, their lovers, their friends—realize moments of true sublimity in the daily activities of life. Perhaps that happens most clearly with Anna Hand who, even as a child, makes memorable moments for her brothers and sisters, and long after her death changes them all profoundly.

Another artist, Ginny Stanford, also figures in *Falling through Space*. Gilchrist writes of buying her first painting from the artist, and the story of the painting and of her relationship with Stanford illustrates how important the visual artist is to the writer. Many of the covers of Gilchrist's books feature Stanford women, young women looking dreamily into an uncertain future. Those women seem to share the dreams of Nora Jane Whittington, Rhoda Manning, and other Gilchrist protagonists. Their freshness overcomes the staleness of the world in which they are often trapped. Stanford's paintings illustrate both the possibilities and the restraints that Gilchrist's characters experience, and they are uncanny in their representation of Gilchrist's themes.

Gilchrist's story of how it took so long to buy a painting from Ginny Stanford turned into a National Public Radio commentary (*FTS*, 75). Gilchrist recounts her attempt to buy a painting from Stanford through Stanford's husband, Frank, and tells how she negotiated the purchase and then became a collector of art as a way of holding to herself moments that endure into eternity. After she had collected for a time, Gilchrist began to give her pieces away and to share them with her children, so that the art she bought was spread all over the southeastern United States. Finally, she sees the act of giving the art to her children as a true sharing, a passing back and forth, a recognition that brings people together. Contrasted to the stale world that Gilchrist says she once chose when she bought a pair of "uncomfortable golden shoes" instead of buying an antique carpenter's bench, the ever-revitalized world of the artist will never "disappear into the destiny of cocktail clothes" (*FTS*, 75).

Still another visual artist—the photographer Clarence John Laughlin, for whom the poem, "The Children of Cheramie Cemetery Terrebonne,

Parish, Louisiana," was written—opened for Gilchrist another avenue for her writing. Gilchrist comments on how Laughlin articulated the relationship between art and the subconscious mind and showed her, through his photographs, "how art takes us past the veils of illusion and returns us to ourselves" (*FTS*, 78). That lesson became, in much of Gilchrist's fiction, the journey that the young women characters take, and Laughlin's articulation of the process helped Gilchrist focus her early work. He also gave her the cover photograph for her first book of poetry. Through her relationships with painters and photographers, Gilchrist came to understand, "They are the best friends a writer has. They teach you to use your eyes" (*FTS*, 82).

Gilchrist also was drawn to scientists and cherished the ideas of Albert Einstein. Were she asked "for a one-sentence biography of Einstein [she] would say he was the freest man [she had] ever known" (*FTS*, 65), precisely because he never compromised: "Nothing was more alien to Einstein than to settle any issue by compromise, in his life or in his science" (*FTS*, 65). For Gilchrist, Einstein's fierce dedication to solutions connects with her own desire to know and with her characters' quest for the truth. Clearly, the title of her collection of short stories *Light Can Be Both Wave and Particle* is a tribute to Einstein.

Another scientist who influenced Gilchrist was Rene Dubos; of him she writes that he changed our notions of humans by focusing on the mystery of life. In doing so, Dubos pointed out that, while "we have been human for a long time, 'the mystery of what makes us so continues to challenge us.' Clearly the first thing we did was probe the mystery and the last thing we will ever do is probe the same mystery" (*FTS*, 69). That mystery, what makes us human and how we live together as humans, resonates throughout Gilchrist's many stories of love and loneliness. Dubos writes of two Neanderthal people who were so crippled that "they must have been completely dependent on the members of their group for a long time" (*FTS*, 69). Their dependence, for Gilchrist, signals the ability of people to help and nurture others, but what of the old people themselves; how did they respond to their dependency? Were they, like Amanda McCamey and Rhoda Manning, always seeking escape? That is the paradox for Gilchrist. When people are dependent, they can call out the very best in others, but their very dependency creates within them the need to be independent. Gilchrist's characters live in communities to assuage their need; they return to families when they are most lonely and alone, but they also struggle fiercely to free themselves from the cloying bonds of love. The two crippled Neanderthals are a paradigm of that paradox.

At the heart of *Falling through Space* is Gilchrist's commentary on writing, especially writing poetry. As a child she exulted in it; it was better than God. It gave her power and dominion. God, on the other hand, "was powerless" (*FTS*, 71). Her further assertion that "God reminded me too much of my father to be in good with me" (*FTS*, 71) hints, once again, at the tension between fathers and daughters throughout her fiction. The young Gilchrist asserted her independence from both God and father, and "poetry took the place of God" (*FTS*, 71). Anne Sexton and Edna St. Vincent Millay spoke to Gilchrist in the "wild lyrical language of the poets"(*FTS*, 72), and Frank Stanford was an important friend and mentor.

The vibrantly lyrical underpinning of Gilchrist's fiction has its origins in her childhood reading, in her friendship with poets, and in her growing appreciation of the visual arts and of artists who "Make It Right" (*FTS*, 77). All influence her writing, and all find their way into her work in her language, in her characters, in her verbal portraits, and in her sense of the community of people trying to find a way to express their humanity.

In Section Three of *Falling through Space,* called "Work," Gilchrist not only outlines a work philosophy that has helped her develop as a writer, but also asserts that work is the only thing that saves the artist. All her artist characters value work in much the same way. Anna Hand returns to writing after a hopeless affair with a married man who will not leave his wife; Amanda McCamey finally realizes that it is work that will free her from her past and from her family sins; and Rhoda Manning, too, finds consolation, hope, and finally, freedom in work. Gilchrist the writer and the characters she creates come to value work not just as therapy but as creative force for change in their lives.

Valuable work contrasts sharply with the meaningless employment that Hollywood represents. Shortly after the successful launching of her first book of short stories, *In the Land of Dreamy Dreams,* Gilchrist was offered "sixty-five thousand dollars to rewrite the Italian film *Wifemistress* and set it in New Orleans." Her response, "Why on earth would you want to do something like that" (*FTS*, 87), is a good indication of the importance of writing in Gilchrist's life. Ever since she was a child, she considered herself a writer, and even when she was not writing, she knew what writing was supposed to be. Hollywood writing is not what writing is supposed to be; "it chews up writers and spits them out. It wastes their time and their dreams" (*FTS*, 88).

The universities, too, come in for criticism in *Falling through Space.* Universities, Gilchrist notes, grasp after the shards of the writers, requesting "letters and notes and worksheets" for their archives, and this causes Gilchrist "to go out to the shed and get a sack of them and burn them up in the wood stove" (*FTS*, 88). She devoted a few National Public Radio talks to the issue of writers' "repressed papers," those writings that lead to stories but are not yet anything more than musings and jottings. Although repressed papers form humorous commentary for National Public Radio, those very papers in Gilchrist's fiction become keys to characters and avenues to freedom. Anna Hand leaves her papers to her sister, who is at first shocked and then liberated by what she finds there. Gilchrist herself does not want her papers cataloged for "some poor graduate student down in a marble basement somewhere going through my notes and letters and wild imaginings" (*FTS*, 88). Family, however, is a different matter.

Within the radio commentaries collected in *Falling through Space* are also the skeletons of characters, incidents, and stories, so if the repressed papers go into Gilchrist's woodstove, the commentaries still give readers a good idea of how the writer shapes fiction. For instance, in one commentary, Gilchrist points out the influence of psychoanalysis on her writing. It helped her to "understand the source of language," and it focused on her own "subconscious motivations and drives" (*FTS*, 90). That understanding certainly strengthens her character development and enables her to look at her fictional world in a way that is both understanding and constructively critical.

The commentaries also gloss the behavior of Gilchrist's characters, and since the behavior of women is a central issue in her fictional world, her observations about herself and the women friends are especially interesting. In addition, they are often quite humorous. Gilchrist frequently looks at herself with the same slightly comic lens that she turns on her fictional families. The issue of fat will never be solved by Rhoda Manning, Helen Hand, Amanda McCamey, and the host of other women who people Gilchrist's fictional universe. The extra pounds that keep them from happiness or that cause male censure are analyzed in terms of a humorous metaphor, but one that also illustrates the deep unhappiness of the women who look at themselves and see bodies that are unacceptable:

> The Castle of Fat is such a problem. The Castle of Fat is surrounded by a moat of self-deception and absurdities. High walls of fantasy surround it. Evil guards of self-hate man the towers. In the square is an everlasting spring of Diet Coke from which the inhabitants draw sustenance. (*FTS*, 96)

The metaphor is particularly appropriate for Gilchrist's women, because they are indeed imprisoned by male conceptions of beauty and femininity. Malcolm and Dudley and Manny and all the other men in Gilchrist's fiction look at their women as property that must be kept up; the way to maintain that property is to keep it beautiful and keep it thin. Women themselves, as Gilchrist finally asserts, must stop accepting a view of themselves that is imposed from without. Of herself, "I can't stand to be dumb and brainwashed about the structure and size of my own body" (*FTS*, 97).

The question posed by another radio commentary is "How much of our so-called body image is fashion" (*FTS*, 102), and that question reasserts the old conflict between what women want for themselves versus what society wants for them. Gilchrist's own response is that "We are diverse and wonderful creatures made of starlight and comet dust. What shape and size our individual bodies take cannot be measured by steel scales and weight charts" (*FTS*, 102–103). That line echoes through much of Gilchrist's fiction as her characters come to see beyond the earthly body and recognize the divine. Those characters increasingly take on, in Gilchrist's descriptive language, the elements of paintings shot through with light and enhanced by the daring exhibited in singular moments of love or courage. Perhaps no one is more like a Ginny Stanford painting than Nora Jane Whittington, who in the course of several stories reveals just the qualities Gilchrist most cherishes in her romantic heroines. Nora Jane can make marvelous leaps of faith that Gilchrist often finds herself incapable of (*FTS*, 91).

Of that wonderful character, Gilchrist also adds, "I created Nora Jane but I have to wait on her to make up her mind before I can finish the title story of my new book [*Light Can Be Both Wave and Particle*]" (*FTS*, 104). Gilchrist sees the connection between her work, her preparation for writing, and her readings in science and philosophy. It is Nora Jane's free will, her sense of her own possibilities, that draws Gilchrist on. In fact, when asked by a reporter about her studies in philosophy, Gilchrist answered, "The effect that studying philosophy has had on my fiction writing is that I know that someday I will get to sit down and write a book about Free Will Versus Determinism and the only character will be me" (*FTS*, 104). That book might well contain a compilation of all Gilchrist's women because her comment describes the essential struggle in the day-to-day life of every one of her female characters. The struggle to assert the self, to take possession of the self, and to love the self is the goal of Rhoda Manning, Amanda McCamey,

Anna Hand, Nora Jane Whittington, and all the other women who people Gilchrist's planet.

Discipline also creates the possibility of getting beyond the writer's block, an affliction from which many writers suffer. Although Gilchrist, in her several discussions about writing for National Public Radio, claims she is very rarely stuck, she also recognizes how the habit of writing balances the wildness of her characters' dreams and helps her to let go and let them speak. She insists that the writer has to "just go right on sitting down at that desk every day no matter how much it seems to be an absurd and useless and boring thing to do"; then, often when the writer least expects it, "the good stuff will suddenly happen" (*FTS,* 105).

Gilchrist's deep belief in her work and in the power of writing to bring order out of chaos even though the chaos keeps "slipping back in" (*FTS,* 128) and her commitment to reading and writing as wedded work are the focus of much of her public radio commentary; they hint at the deeply philosophical foundation of all her fiction. Quoting Bertrand Russell during an address at commencement exercises at the University of Arkansas, Gilchrist spoke to the graduates of three tools to enrich their lives: love, knowledge, and pity. All three do, indeed, permeate every page of her work, give meaning to existence, and hold the chaos at bay. The quest for love is a journey toward community, a way, as many of Gilchrist's characters attest, of not being alone in the world. The quest for knowledge is related to love, for it is within that quest that Gilchrist, and Russell, think that understanding grows. Finally, however, it is "pity for the suffering of mankind" that focuses human existence, because pity challenges the suffering and torment that "make a mockery of what human life should be." As Russell said, "I long to alleviate the evil but I cannot and I too suffer" (*FTS,* 160). That challenge to the graduates is also Gilchrist's challenge to herself as a writer to understand what each individual experiences and to empathize.

Throughout her fiction, the need to love and to know enlivens and enriches her characters and challenges them to press on in their romantic quests for wholeness. Gilchrist herself jokes that when she sits down to create characters they grab their own lives and insist on telling their own stories. "Minor characters get up off the page and take the pen out of my hand and start expanding their roles" (*FTS,* 126). Gilchrist says, "In a way my characters are right. I can see their point. I have a responsibility to Freddy Harwood to let him tell his side of the story and not just leave him sitting in a hot tub with a broken heart" (*FTS,* 126). So Freddy, too, wants to love and to know. He, too, can suffer and feel pity

for others' suffering. Gilchrist's fiction tells, over and over, the story of
the human quest, not just Freddy's, and that is why, for Gilchrist, "there
may be a limited number of characters any one writer can create and
perhaps a limited number of stories any writer can tell" (*FTS*, 126). At
its best, the story of love and suffering is the human story.

Gilchrist's National Public Radio talks reach out beyond the pages of
her journals to speak of her past, her family, her writing, and her every-
day concerns. *Falling through Space* also contains several magazine articles
that capture her sense of adventure. An article included from *Southern
Living*, on searching for the source of the White River in the mountains
of Arkansas, and a piece about men, "Sons and Brothers and Husbands
and Lovers, Or, Why I Am Not a Feminist," both echo many of the sentiments of female characters from Gilchrist's novels and short stories.
Who but Gilchrist's own brother Dooley could have been the model for
Rhoda's brother Dudley? Gilchrist observes in her "Sons and Brothers"
article, much as Rhoda opines about Dudley, "My mother liked him best
and my father liked him best and my paternal grandmother liked him
best. He was always getting his Eagle Scout badge or going to the
Junior Olympics or stoking the furnace or carrying out the garbage or
being brave when he put out his eye" (*FTS*, 152). What sister, or fictional sister, would not be both jealous of and in love with such a
paragon of a brother? Gilchrist points out about him and other men,
"All my life they have protected me and I believe they will go on doing
it as long as I love them in return" (*FTS*, 152). So in the end, all relationships come down to loving and returning love, and all her stories
seek that end as well. *Falling through Space*, taken as a whole, illuminates
the process of living and writing and loving.

Myth

Anabasis

In *Falling through Space*, Gilchrist talks about a novel in progress that she
says she thought was finished. Then, suddenly, she says she "realized it
was an illusion that the novel was finished . . . it would take several
more years and two or three more drafts to finish it" (*FTS*, 127). This
story eventually became the novel *Anabasis*. Gilchrist went back to the
work and did indeed take several more years to finish it. In her journal,
she describes the book as "a novel set in Greece during the Pelopon-
nesian Wars. My pet book, based on a story I made up when I was a

child . . ."(*FTS,* 127). It is the result, she says, of her decision to become a scholar, and it is important because it illustrates the basis of much of her fiction set in contemporary society:

> I will write a novel set in ancient Greece, I told myself. Anyone can do anything, and I am going down the hill and go to the library and take out every book ever written about ancient Greece and read them and then I'm going over to Daniel Levine's office and borrow all his books and then I'll sign up for Greek classes and I will spend as many years as it takes. I want to be a great and honored writer, a scholar, a serious and noble person (*FTS,* 134).

Although the tone of Gilchrist's resolution might be somewhat self-mocking and ironic, her research, combined with the memory of her childhood story, resulted in the novel *Anabasis,* published in 1994. It is the tale of a slave girl who escapes her servitude and begins an almost epic journey toward self-knowledge. Symbolic in nature, the story is a magical narrative of growth, discovery, and finally, love. Greece in 431 B.C., the setting for the novel, was at the end of its Golden Age, and Gilchrist sees parallels with the late twentieth century. America, too, is at the end of a Golden Age; the hope and promise of democracy is also threatened by people's indifference and by powerful cartels as it was in Greece more than two thousand years ago. The story of the slave girl and her quest for freedom and understanding is an allegory for modern times.

All the themes of Gilchrist's contemporary stories find their way into *Anabasis.* A southern writer writing about slavery inevitably invites comparisons with the antebellum South, and early in the novel, the slave girl Auria is in much the same position as a young black girl might have been in the America of slavery. She is just reaching womanhood, and "her breasts [are] beginning and her hips widening."[4] The philosopher Philokrates, to whom the servant girl has been assigned, knows Auria's fate and fears it. Once her maturity is noticed, her master Meldrus will give her to someone for pleasure and for Meldrus's own purposes. The philosopher has tried to give Auria some resources against the future: "He had taught her his knowledge of herbs and he had done a more dangerous thing. He had taught her to read and write" (*An,* 3–4). Although fathers, brothers, and husbands are supposed to protect women and girls, Philokrates realizes that he cannot protect Auria from the inevitable, and Gilchrist is aware of the dark side of the compact between women and men. Women's devotion and love does not often spare them the harsh realities that men are supposed to shield them from.

The fate that the philosopher fears occurs, and all his knowledge cannot guard Auria from it. Raped one evening by Polymion, a traveling merchant to whom she has been traded for some coins, she learns that "a man takes pleasure of a woman's body and returns darkness and sorrow, pain and fear, bitterness and burning" (An, 23). Her introduction to brutal sex awakens her resolve that she will not be a slave for life, and after the death of Philokrates, Auria plans her own escape.

The death of Auria's mentor and guardian is important in Gilchrist's vision of the relationship between fathers and daughters. Fathers are supposed to protect daughters, and when they can't, they fail at their most essential task. Just as Dudley Manning and the men of the Hand clan must protect their women, Philokrates must protect Auria from men who would abuse her. His failure to do that, more than his age, is what kills him. He has lost his purpose in life.

Auria is strengthened in her resolve to escape her enslavement when she sees another slave putting an infant girl out in the cold for the wolves to devour. Auria, determined not to let the child die, takes over the role of the protector and rescues her from the cave where she has been put to perish. With the infant girl, whom she names Kleis, she begins her journey. Gilchrist sees, in Auria's resolve and in her ability to survive the assault on her virginity, images of her modern heroines. They, too, must survive the assaults of the modern world, and they, too, often find themselves enslaved to husbands who do not value them for anything but their bodies (often criticizing them if they are too fat) and to children whose constant demands undermine their mothers' quest for freedom. However, Gilchrist notes in her interview with Kay Bonetti that her children and grandchildren are more important to her than anything else in the world, and therefore that entrapment is at least partially blessed. Auria could simply flee, but she sees in the child left out to die an image of an earlier possibility in her own life. Why are daughters not valued, she wonders, and determines that she will save the child just as she will save herself.

Like many of Gilchrist's later heroines, Auria is self-reflective and self-conscious. She speaks to the creatures she has fled with—the child, a dog, and a goat—saying, "Nothing can harm us. I, Auria, the fearless, lead us" (An, 40). That defiant tone and attitude is central to Gilchrist's romantic heroines such as Amanda McCamey, Rhoda Manning, and

Nora Jane Whittington. Like Alisha Terrebone in an early Gilchrist short story, Auria seems to view her life as if it were a play. Many of Gilchrist's characters view themselves as characters in their own dramas, and Auria, too, is creating a romantic escape much like Nora Jane's from New Orleans. Her quest takes on mythical proportions through the power of her imagination and through her will to succeed.

The physical journey into the mountains is also a psychological journey couched in the guise of a philosophical quest. Gilchrist has often said that she is a philosopher and a poet, and her philosophical bent is given free rein in *Anabasis*. The philosopher spirit of Philokrates resides in the newborn child, and Auria must save his wisdom just as she must nourish and protect the child. As she journeys deeper and deeper into the interior of the country and of her own mind, a new meaning of life opens before her.

Understanding and spiritual growth come to Auria. She finds in a hidden valley a hut made by a man named Clarius, who led his father's slaves in revolt and escaped to the valley to hide. Eventually, he left his hiding place and spent his life seeking freedom and equality for Athenians who did not wish to accept the rising dictatorship of Cleon. The writings he leaves in the hut nourish Auria's spirit just as his garden nourishes and strengthens her body. Finally, all these lives come together in the secret camp of the escaped slaves. That camp, where Auria eventually takes the child, is boldly described in Clarius's writings: "HERE IS A PLACE WHERE THEY WILL NOT KILL A MAN FOR ASKING QUESTIONS" (*An*, 51). Clarius's hut and the camp are the havens of those who do not love slavery and who will not accept that one person should have ownership of another.

As with all of Gilchrist's characters, Auria's quest for freedom leads her away from the only family she has ever known. The death of Philokrates leaves her essentially an orphan, and even though she has the child Kleis to care for in the hut in the hidden valley, she is cut off from humanity. The loneliness she feels echoes across the centuries and resonates in Gilchrist's modern women. Auria is "filled with a sense of how alone she was, how far away from the world where men and women ate together in the evenings and played music and danced in a circle and told each other their dreams" (*An*, 59). But she also understands that her loneliness is the price she pays for her freedom, and she will never be a slave; "I will kill loneliness. I will never go back" (*An*, 51), she vows.

Into her refuge comes another escaped slave, Meion, who was enslaved when his city was defeated by the Athenians. His father was killed by the invaders, and his mother was sold into slavery. His escape from his master leads him to the mountains where the army of runaway slaves is gathering to prepare a rebellion against the slaveholders of Athens. He finds Auria in the hidden valley and offers to take her and the baby to the mountain camp. On that journey, Auria begins to understand love. Her first winter in the hut was marked by loneliness, but Meion's arrival signals the birth of love.

Freedom, loneliness, love, and finally, self-discovery: Auria experiences all these emotions and grows into a powerful member of the band of runaway slaves. She also meets Clarius, the maker of the hut that saved her life, and sees in his dreams of freedom ideals to match her own. She grows, during the course of the novel, from a young girl whose knowledge has never been tested into a self-reliant and courageous young woman. Auria is, in fact, an ideal heroine, one whom many of Gilchrist's modern characters would do well to emulate, and she illustrates the writer's ability to turn a romantic childhood story into a philosophical meditation on the very subjects that Gilchrist's modern-day stories try to encompass. The nature of the individual, alone and in community; the nature of love, as demanded by a master and as won by a lover; and the responsibility that people have to others: Auria learns to understand all these ideas, and she comes to know what freedom really means once she is very close to losing it again.

Illuminations

Gilchrist's poetry, her journals, and her philosophical novel enrich and illuminate her other work. Although essentially a short-story writer and novelist of contemporary society, Gilchrist is able, through her other writings, to test, question, and develop the philosophical underpinnings of her fiction. She goes back again and again to the central questions of her work. The pressure of the past, whether it be an idealized childhood or a past that blights the present, forges the strong core of much of her writing. The tension between the desire to escape and the need for attachment as well as the ambivalence in relationships of all kinds, especially sexual relationships, enriches her writing and gives her characters depth and complexity. Gilchrist's handling of the dynamics of the father-daughter relationship, so well described in the poetry and in *Anabasis,* informs and critiques all the families she writes about. The importance of artistic endeavor in focusing women's identities and enriching their lives is central to many of Gilchrist's most fully developed characters, and Gilchrist's own progress as a writer is most thoroughly analyzed in *Falling through Space*. The wonderfully human, comic, independent women of her stories are given added depth through the radio commentaries. It is in the commentaries and in the early poems that the progenitors of her fictional characters are found. Finally, Gilchrist speaks of the darker side of human experience, the possibility that people will use others unfairly, will take advantage of innocence, or will simply not return love; that fear germinates in the poetry and journals and matures in Gilchrist's fiction.

Chapter Three
The Short Stories

To date, Ellen Gilchrist has published five collections of short stories and a book of three novellas that link her short-story techniques with her novels. The short stories are connected by characters who recur from the earliest work, *In the Land of Dreamy Dreams,* to the most recent, *The Courts of Love.* She has also collected all the stories about her character Rhoda Manning in a book entitled *Rhoda: A Life in Stories.* Taken together, her stories form a view of life that has developed consistently throughout her fiction, and Gilchrist has worked to create a sense of wholeness in the stories, a world view that has come more to the forefront with the publication of each new collection. It is in the short stories that Gilchrist's view of women, her ideas of the artist, and her critique of the South most clearly emerge. Further, her method of storytelling, characterized by a humorous, gossipy style anchored in a hidden sadness, has been honed to a fine art in the course of her career.

In the Land of Dreamy Dreams

After the University of Arkansas Press published *In the Land of Dreamy Dreams* in 1981, Ellen Gilchrist was heralded as a new southern voice. Her collection was an immediate success, selling out its first printing and making Ellen Gilchrist's name a household word in New Orleans, where many of the stories take place. So popular was the book that Little, Brown bought the rights to it and reprinted it in 1985, giving Gilchrist a contract for a novel and another collection of short stories.

In the Land of Dreamy Dreams is both an introduction to many characters who reappear throughout Gilchrist's body of work and a coherent set of stories that comment trenchantly on southern women's lives. Eleven of the 14 stories are told in women's voices or viewed through women's perspectives. The stories portray a world that is at once fetid and fecund. In many cases, by setting her stories in New Orleans, Gilchrist unveils the personal and social corruption of that particular southern society. She is, however, far more interested in how females of all ages find their voices in a world that tries to keep them mute and complacent than she is in simply uncovering social stagnation and decay. She returns again and again to the South, and particularly to New Orleans, for her settings because, like many regional writers before her, she "cannot resist the descriptions of setting, landscapes, dialects and societies which, love them or not, are easily recognizable as home."[1]

Gilchrist balances her keen interest in her female characters by opening the collection with a story entitled "Rich," which focuses on a married couple who are, at the beginning of the story, just another blissfully rich New Orleans couple. In this story, which won the prestigious Pushcart Prize, the protagonist Tom Wilson is a man who suffers tragedy in his personal life, loses a good deal of money, falls from favor with New Orleans society, and finally, commits suicide after killing his adopted daughter, Helen, who the whole town assumes really was his child. More to Gilchrist's point, he also shoots an expensive Labrador retriever, an act his social equals find hard to fathom. It is, in fact, more acceptable that Tom destroyed his daughter, a thorn in the family side since her adoption, than it is that he carelessly dispatched an expensive dog. As the introductory story in the book, "Rich" highlights two important themes for Gilchrist: the perils of wealth and the fall from grace.

Structurally, the story separates the Wilsons from the world of the have-nots: "Tom and Letty Wilson were rich in everything" (*DD*, 3). According to the narrator, they also had the good fortune of "knowing exactly who they were" (*DD*, 3), a comment riddled with Gilchrist's ironic point of view. In fact, self-knowledge is in short supply in many of Gilchrist's characters, and the shock of self-awareness can often be devastating, as it is for Tom. Although Tom and Letty's marriage is introduced as perfectly happy, an undercurrent of evil contaminates this apparently unblemished existence. During his senior year at Tulane University, Tom was responsible for an accidental death in a hazing incident at the Southern Yacht Club. Tom's reaction reveals the darker side of his personality: "He had never liked the boy and had suspected him of being involved with queers and nigger lovers who hung around the philosophy department and the school newspaper" (*DD*, 6). That death gives a context to the final scene of the novel. The conflict between the romantic vision of love that Tom's rich young wife has is craftily contrasted with the reality behind the illusions. Even in her first book of stories, Gilchrist shows her awareness of the pull that social status has for her characters, and she seems to watch with detachment as Letty and Tom's world collapses. That collapse is seen both as a loss of the luck they so assured themselves they were entitled to and a fall from grace, an expulsion from Eden. Others in her social circle cannot believe that "that much bad luck could happen to a nice lady like Letty Dufrechou Wilson, who never hurt a flea or gave anyone a minute's trouble in her life" (*DD*, 23).

Gilchrist, even in this early story, has complete control over description. The climactic passage on the shooting of the child Helen and the expensive Labrador is the hallmark of Gilchrist's approach to her characters. They might feel their predicament very keenly, but the authorial intelligence sees them in a larger picture and that larger vision is what controls the tone: "[Helen's] thick body rolled across the hardwood floor and lodged against a hat rack from Jody Mellon's old office in the Hibernia Bank Building. One of her arms landed on a pile of old *Penthouse* magazines and her disordered brain flung its roses north and east and south and west and rejoined the order from which it casually arose" (*DD*, 33). In that passage, Gilchrist is not prepared to take her characters as seriously as they take themselves. Or, as in Helen's case, Gilchrist is not prepared to grieve for a completely unsympathetic character, even a child. Her cool lack of sentimentality rings in the impersonal dispersal of Helen's brains. While New Orleans society ostensibly mourns Tom's death and grieves for Letty's bad luck, "no one . . . wanted to believe a man would shoot a $3,000 Labrador retriever sired by Super Chief out of Prestidigitation" (*DD*, 23). The child's death is not even mentioned, much less mourned.

The introductory story sets the tone for much of the book. Gilchrist sets up, in the marriage of Tom and Letty, the value system she then attacks. She realizes that there is a fatal attraction for that world and its values, even in herself, but she is able, in her fiction, to create sufficient distance to see the snake in the garden.

Gilchrist looks with a sardonic eye on the behavior of all her characters, not just those whose fall from grace might be considered tragic. Alisha Terrebone, the rich, bored divorcée of "There's a Garden of Eden," accepts the failure of love as her new young lover, Michael, rows her through a New Orleans flood to her mother's doorstep: "This is the very last time I will ever love anyone she told herself. I will love this boy until he leaves me. And then I will never love another human being" (*DD*, 47). Of course, Michael will leave Alisha; that is the other side of the romantic coin that Gilchrist has flipped. The writer is aware of Alisha's need for the self-dramatizing moment of the quest as her character sits "in the bow [of the rowboat] and [writes] a script for herself" (*DD*, 47). Gilchrist's final comment, "and then she went to work to make it all come true" (*DD,* 47), allows the author both to distance herself from Alisha and to comment on the failure of the character to come to terms with reality. However, unlike the debacle of Tom and Letty, the aging of Alisha Terrebone is gently humorous rather than bitingly satiric. Gilchrist at once creates the notion of romantic love and undercuts it with her wry attitude toward the character experiencing it. She is delineating the aging southern belle as she peals the death knell of the species.

It is also in *In the Land of Dreamy Dreams* that Gilchrist introduces characters who will grow in importance as the body of her work grows. Nora Jane Whittington, who debuts in "The Famous Poll at Jody's Bar," is perhaps Gilchrist's most endearing renegade. She is a young woman who robs Jody's bar, "the oldest neighborhood bar in the Irish Channel section of New Orleans" (*DD,* 53). At the time Nora Jane decides to rob the bar, Wesley Labouisse, a regular, is conducting a poll to determine whether Prescott Hamilton IV, another regular, should get married. "He and Emily Anne had been getting along fine for years without getting married, and he didn't see what difference his moving into Emily Anne's house at this late date was going to make in the history of the world" (*DD,* 55). Prescott will bow to the will of the poll; only one man has to advise him to marry and he will do so. While the men—Jody, Wesley, Prescott, and the judge, who is also in the bar drinking—count the ballots from the poll, Nora Jane enters the bar brandishing a gun, locks them all in the ladies' room, and makes off with the cash. She then changes into a nun's habit and leaves to make her way to her lover who is waiting for her in San Jose. As she leaves the bar, Nora Jane drops her ballot in the box, shifting the frame of the story once again. Gilchrist's control of irony in the story is heightened by Nora Jane's last act, and the reader is left to puzzle over the outcome of the poll.

It is clear in the story that none of the men, despite any protests to the contrary, has any idea of how to deal with women. For Wesley, Jody, Prescott, and the judge, all women are like Emily Anne, Prescott Hamilton IV's fiancée; they are to be humored but never allowed to interfere with the business of men's lives. Nora Jane baffles them all and makes a mockery of their masculinity by locking them in the ladies' room.

Nora Jane Whittington manages to remain undefeated by her alcoholic mother and the mesdames of the Sacred Heart, the nuns to whom she has been sent for her education. She relentlessly holds to her notion of romantic escape; in fact, according to Margaret Schramm, "her romanticism and her capacity for self-delusion are underscored in the ending of the story, when she begins her journey to Sandy," her ne'er-do-well boyfriend.[2] Nora Jane, in her early incarnations, is similar to Alisha Terrebone in her capacity to script her own life despite the obstacles that reality places in her path; however, she is far more endearing in her pursuit of romantic love.

On the other hand, LaGrande McGruder, the central character in the title story, is no romantic. She confronts reality and is defeated by it. A true daughter of the Confederacy and heiress to all the privilege that New Orleans society has to offer, LaGrande plays tennis "four or five hours a day whenever it wasn't raining or she didn't have a funeral to attend" (DD, 60). In a tennis match that replays the Civil War, LaGrande cheats Roxanne Miller, "that goddamn little new-rich Yankee bitch," out of a tennis victory. Her deliberate bad call is a result of her assessment of her opponent: "she had looked across the net at the impassive face of the interloper who was about to humiliate her at her own tennis club and she had changed her mind about honor quicker than the speed of light" (DD, 61).

LaGrande McGruder and Roxanne Miller are locked in more than a ferocious tennis match. They represent opposing forces in the war for the South. LaGrande, the old southerner, has all the prejudices and narrowness of vision that the upper class is heir to. Even Claiborne Redding, her father's old doubles partner, feels, as he observes the match, "the entire culture of the white Christian world to be stretched out on some sort of endless Maginot Line besieged by the children of the poor carrying portable radios and boxes of fried chicken" (DD, 70). He sees LaGrande cheat and accepts it as a part of what is needed to save this world. Like LaGrande, "he had been a party to a violation of a code he had lived by all his life" (DD, 70). Yet he could still sit at the tennis club and sip his coffee without regret.

Roxanne Miller represents the interloper. Although she is not poor, she has the grasping and acquisitive values that LaGrande sees as characteristic of those not born to her kind of money and to the southern code of gentility. Roxanne is pushy, unpleasant, and slightly crippled as well as unattractive. She is also Jewish, a fact that is lost on neither LaGrande nor Claiborne.

If the reader is tempted to side with the underdog, Roxanne, against the established order, Gilchrist prevents that by making her so unattractive. "She had spent thousands of dollars on private tennis lessons, hun-

dreds of dollars on equipment, and untold time and energy giving cocktail parties and dinner parties for the entrenched players who one by one
she had courted and blackmailed and finagled into giving her matches
and return matches until finally one day she would catch them at a
weak moment and defeat them" (*DD*, 61). LaGrande has successfully
avoided her for quite a while before she is caught having to grant Roxanne a match, and that match has finally led LaGrande to throw her
tennis racket into the Mississippi River and vow to "quit playing tennis
forever" (*DD*, 60).

Roxanne may seem to have taken over the Tennis Club, but, as
LaGrande grumbles to herself, "at least they don't let Jews into the
country club yet. At least that's still sacred" (*DD*, 61). The irony of
LaGrande's comment about the sacredness is that it, too, is shallow and
vacuous. In LaGrande, Gilchrist portrays the failure of the South to
grow and accept outsiders, but she also criticizes many of those outsiders
who do not enrich but rather debase the world they take over.

"Indignities" also pictures the decaying world of New Orleans.
Melissa is the daughter of a rich, New Orleans society matron. Her
mother has had a double mastectomy and then shows her friends the
scars of her absent breasts at a dinner at Antoine's, a posh French Quarter restaurant. Melissa has to confront her mother's illness and death
while her mother plans her own funeral and imagines that she is going
to meet friends. The macabre nature of Melissa's mother's behavior indicates the older woman's real unwillingness to see the decay and disease
in her own body and in her world.

"Suicides" has the same sinister tone as "Indignities." In this story,
the characters waiting for death are twin brothers. Each commits suicide. The first to do so is Joshua Treadway. He "just walked out one
night and dumped himself into the Puget Sound" (*DD*, 75). The story
would be little more than a gothic story of twinship and death, except
that Gilchrist refers to Joshua's suicide again in the title story of the collection *Light Can Be Both Wave and Particle* and in that piece, love overcomes the sadness of loss.

Rhoda Manning: An Introduction

Five of the stories in *In the Land of Dreamy Dreams*—"1957, A
Romance," "Generous Pieces," "Revenge," "1944," and "Perils of the
Nile"—focus on Rhoda Manning, a character whom readers follow
throughout several Gilchrist collections from her childhood through her

stormy adolescence into adulthood, love, marriage, affairs, and career. Rhoda has appeared in all of Gilchrist's short-story collections and grows with each publication, emerging as a fully developed character in the novel *Net of Jewels*. She is not the only character to appear again and again, but she becomes one of the most completely realized. In the earliest stories, Rhoda is at once a sharp commentator on the other people in her family and deeply influenced by her own romantic conceptions of how the world ought to be. Like Nora Jane and Alisha, Rhoda, too, "always believed her own stories as soon as she told them" (*DD*, 82).

Born in the South, Rhoda is transplanted to Indiana during the Second World War. Her father is a successful engineer who adapts easily to northern life, but her mother, Ariane, a University of Georgia cheerleader who "was voted Most Popular Girl" when she was a senior (*DD*, 97), cannot stand "this insane life in this hick Yankee town" (*DD*, 102). None of Ariane Manning's charm protects her from the hostile forces that attack her and her family. Her husband has an affair, her son loses an eye in a childhood accident, and worst of all, her daughter is not always under her protective gaze. Rhoda's mother complains, "I don't know who she's with half the time. God knows who she plays with. God knows what she's doing" (*DD*, 102). The closely knit southern family—the cousins, aunts, uncles, and family servants—disappears with the war and with the family's move to the North. That move frees Rhoda to explore the world at will, to choose her friends, and to achieve a certain distance from her family, but she is also lonely and has none of the comforts of the southern community.

In "Revenge," Rhoda and her brother are at home in Mississippi, and surrounded by cousins and a very southern grandmother, Rhoda is expected to act the part of a young southern lady. Of this story, which was the beginning of the Rhoda stories, Gilchrist said: "That was the first time I wrote in Rhoda Manning's voice and as soon as I typed the line I knew the little girl as I know myself" (*R*, vii–viii). The voice of that little girl is vociferous in her indignity at the injustice perpetrated upon her, and Rhoda continues, throughout the many stories in which she appears, to be the voice of women's anger at their lot. Not allowed by her boy cousins to participate in the building of a broad jump pit to prepare for the Olympics, Rhoda must be content to be her cousin's maid of honor. Lauralee Manning, "widowed at the beginning of the war when her young husband crashed his Navy training plane into the Pacific" (*DD*, 117), joined the WAVES and left the Delta to serve as a secretary to an admiral in Pensacola, Florida. Suddenly, she returns home to announce she is going to marry a Unitarian real estate developer. In this story, Rhoda gains small revenge against her brother and cousins by taking center stage at Lauralee's wedding, but her real achievement is her pole vault, accomplished while the wedding guests are shouting her name. Rhoda's success in her jump is a revenge upon her brother and cousins, but its effect—her momentary triumph and euphoria—might well sour her for further experience. Rhoda, at the age of 10, lies in the sawdust, very still, waiting for her family to rush across the field toward her. A later observation, "Sometimes I think whatever has happened since has been of no real interest to me" (*DD*, 124), puts an entire life into depressing perspective.

A related story, "Traveler," features LeLe, Leland Louise Arnold, a southern girl trapped in Indiana, a girl whose dreams of success at Franklin Junior High are shattered by her failure to be elected cheerleader. In this story, Gilchrist ascribes many of Rhoda's physical characteristics and much of her personality to LeLe, who may be an evolutionary step as Gilchrist tests and elaborates the character of Rhoda. Rhoda has already taken on a distinct personality in the collection and has a streak of willfulness and a steely determination. LeLe falters in her determination to create a wonderful background for herself by telling patent lies to her southern cousin and her cousin's friends. In her desire to be accepted yet seen as slightly foreign and "Yankee," LeLe makes up stories of a college sweetheart with thyroid cancer (a part of Rhoda's life story as well) and of success in cheerleading (even though she did not actually make the squad). LeLe wants to be seen as "a girl who would do anything" (*DD*, 144) and is elated when she overhears someone compare her to Zelda Fitzgerald. That comparison is made by "a summer visitor from Washington, D.C." (*DD*, 144) and speaks as much to Leland's ignorance (she is not sure who Zelda Fitzgerald was) as it does to the ironic overlay of the story. In actuality, Leland Louise Arnold is an overweight adolescent who, no matter what her self-perception is, must return with her parents to Indiana at the end of the summer and will be remembered by her southern companions not for her daring but for the extra ten pounds she must shed to be "a really beautiful girl" (*DD*, 147).

Victory over Japan

In the Land of Dreamy Dreams not only acts as an introduction to recurring characters and themes that Gilchrist builds on over the course of her several novels and short-story collections but also sets the stage for characters whose importance becomes increasingly evident as each new book appears. *Victory over Japan,* published in 1984, picks up Gilchrist's emerging character, Rhoda Manning, and devotes the first section of the book, "Rhoda," to three stories about her: "Victory over Japan," "Music," and "The Lower Garden District Free Gravity Mule Blight or Rhoda, a Fable." As in the previous collection, the stories show Rhoda as a young girl, an adolescent, and a young wife. In these stories, her character is more fully fleshed out, and the conflicts in her life become much more intense. Her inability to find happiness and fulfillment in the traditional roles of mother and wife are starkly highlighted in "Rhoda, a Fable." There is a glibness in the manner with which Rhoda goes about freeing herself of her unwanted husband, Jody Wells. She dreams that she is crushing his skull and wakes feeling "purged of evil" (*VOJ,* 52). Her scenario for the divorce is, as she calculates it, "easy as pie. . . . All you needed was money. All you needed for anything was money" (*VOJ,* 52–53). Rhoda's vision of her future carries Gilchrist's ironic comment on the lives of the New Orleans wealthy. Rhoda believes that everything is easy. Having spent her childhood in the North, she has not yet really been stifled by the rigid strictures of the Old South; they have glanced off her frantically imaginative psyche.

Gilchrist, however, is all too aware of the disparity between the freedom Rhoda assumes as entitlement and the world in which she is trying to achieve it. The second section of the book opens with a story called "Looking over Jordan," which illustrates the world that Rhoda will come to know. Lady Margaret Sarpie, a character in the story, learns all too disastrously that the world exacts its price. "Being poor and living in a shotgun apartment wasn't working out. It was terrible. It wasn't working out. Nothing was working out" (*VOJ,* 77). Lady Margaret wants to be hip, to sit in Tipitina's with Homer Davis and pretend that her father, the brigadier general, hasn't really been a part of the Old South, hasn't participated in the oppression of people like Homer Davis. Yet Davis himself sees through Lady Margaret's pose and turns to her and challenges, "what do you want to hear now, white lady? . . . What do you want Homer Davis to play for you now?" (*VOJ,* 78).

The tension in the story is further heightened when Lady Margaret and her cousin, Devoie Denery, arrive at the family vacation home in Mandeville. There, Lady Margaret encounters Anna Hand, the writer whose book, *The Assumption,* she has just pilloried in the *Times Picayune.* Hand, however, has no idea who Lady Margaret is and obviously doesn't read reviews. Her world is the world of the artist. It is, in fact, the world Lady

Margaret would like to be a part of. The artist has managed to negotiate the distance between the Old and New South in a way that respects what is best in the past while creating a world that values creative activity and gender freedom. Lady Margaret cannot understand what Anna Hand has written precisely because she cannot understand the writer's quest for a self free of social strictures. Anna's art represents a freedom that is supported by enormous discipline while Lady Margaret's idea of freedom is simply a form of license, a form of laissez-faire given to her by a society that is attached to "faded gentility and remembered glamour."[3] Furthermore, Anna Hand is one of Gilchrist's many thinly disguised autobiographical portraits, and *The Assumption* is certainly a reference to Gilchrist's own first novel, *The Annunciation*. Anna, the writer as the voice of the family, the community, and the South, will appear again and again in Gilchrist's stories and novels, and she will always challenge the silly, empty traditions of a South that is both dead and destructive.

Lady Margaret's vacuity pales beside the emptiness of Diane and Lanier, who, in "The Gauzy Edge of Paradise," spend their lives going on diets. Their trip to the coast to lose weight and their subsequent tryst with Diane's cousin Sandor illuminate the empty center of their lives. The taxi driver who robs them and ties them up acts as an almost comic interruption of the ménage à trois that isn't going well. The only thing left for the three to do is to go back to the beach house and make chocolate milkshakes.

In two stories in the third section of *Victory over Japan,* Gilchrist brings back Nora Jane Whittington. An author's note in *Victory over Japan* reminds readers of the character's earlier appearance in "The Famous Poll at Jody's Bar," where she robbed the bar and headed off for California to meet her lover, Sandy George Wade. As Gilchrist points out in her note, "I wish I could say that Sandy was waiting at the airport when she got there, sleepless and excited and true. I wish that dreams came true, that courage and tenderness were rewarded in the world as they should be" (*VOJ*, 145). That romantic notion is undercut both by Sandy's failure to make the dream come true and by the four earthquakes that shake the Bay Area and Nora Jane's confidence in the world as she has known it. Nora Jane is, however, a survivor, and Sandy's absence leaves room for her to fall in love with, or at least fall in with, Freddy Harwood, bookshop owner and incurable romantic, who falls head over heels in love with her.

Related to Nora Jane's freewheeling lifestyle is Gilchrist's literary style. As Dean Flower said in a 1985 review of *Victory over Japan* for the

Hudson Review, "the distinctive trait of Gilchrist's colloquial style is its deliberate naïveté."[4] Certainly, what Flower terms "deliberate naïveté" precisely matches Nora Jane's state of mind. Unlike many of the society debs whom Gilchrist shows as clinging to an untenable social position, Nora Jane makes her own life and lives, as she says, "getting into destiny" (*VQJ,* 189).

Nora Jane is also on the margins of society. Her robbery in "The Famous Poll at Jody's Bar" has put her on the fringes of the world she grew up in. Gilchrist offers her as a contrast to the shallowness of the characters who are central to New Orleans society. Her Robin Hood–like venture both mocks and takes advantage of the society from which many of Gilchrist's characters come. As J. Randall Woodland has pointed out in *Louisiana Women Writers,* many of Gilchrist's characters "inhabit the margins of this society" (Brown, 196), and in doing so, they comment on and critique that world, noticing its shallowness and its meaningless rituals.

Nora Jane, in her flight from New Orleans, is looking for a new world. Her quest is for romance, a romance she could not find in a city that denied it to anyone outside a certain narrow social class; instead she faces new responsibilities when she finds herself pregnant. As her friend Tam tells her when Nora Jane comes to Tam for help after discovering she is going to have a baby, "Start at the beginning. Tell story all over. Leave out romance" (*VQJ,* 185). However, Nora Jane could never leave out romance; that is the essence of her life. In telling the story, Nora Jane reveals Gilchrist's ability to match character with style. Nora Jane's story is straightforward and humorous, but her voice and concerns are never lost. Nora Jane finds herself pregnant and alone in California with only Tam and Li Suyin for company. Freddy Harwood, rich bookstore owner and hopelessly romantic lover of Nora Jane, would marry her immediately if he knew of the baby, and Sandy, the deadbeat lover, would probably run, but neither can help Nora Jane. They are too concerned with their own perceptions of events. The Chinese couple, to whom Nora Jane is teaching English, see the event in terms of probability. Li determines that there is a 46 percent chance the baby is Freddy's and a 54 percent chance that it is fathered by Sandy. But percentages aside, the two embryos (for Nora Jane has conceived twins) "Lydia and Tammili Whittington settled down and went to sleep" (*VQJ,* 187) in Nora Jane's womb, resting up for their spectacular entrance in a future Gilchrist book.

The story of Nora Jane's pregnancy is fraught with chance events that add to the unreality of the situation but also reveal Gilchrist's talent for capturing the essence of characters. Nora Jane, trapped on a San Francisco bridge during an earthquake, helps a woman who was car-pooling a group of children. The interchange among the children and between the children and Nora Jane, reveals the "deliberate naïveté" of which Flower speaks in his review. Confronting the frightened children, Nora Jane says, "NOW ALL OF YOU SHUT UP A MINUTE . . . This is an emergency. When you have an emergency everybody has to stick together and act right. . . . So, if you'll be quiet and act like big people I will sing to you. I happen to be a wonderful singer" (*VOJ,* 201). She enters their world and draws them out by singing "Walt Disney and *Jesus Christ Superstar* and Janis Joplin musicals" (*VOJ,* 202). She has moved as far as it is possible to move from the stuffy New Orleans Academy of the Most Sacred Heart where she had been "the despair of the sisters . . . because she would never use her voice for the glory of God. . . . All Nora Jane had ever used her voice for was to memorize phonograph albums in case there was a war and all the stereos were blown up" (*VOJ,* 202). The bridge in San Francisco is a far cry from the world of Mardi Gras, the Momus and Comus balls, and the Southern Yacht Club, all heralds of the jaded aristocracy of a dying New Orleans.

In the fourth section of *Victory over Japan,* entitled "Crystal," Gilchrist introduces Traceleen, another marginal character, who works for Crystal Weiss and whose comments on uptown New Orleans society are both trenchant and humorous. Gilchrist modeled Traceleen after the black woman Rosalie Davis to whom she dedicated *In the Land of Dreamy Dreams,* and both Rosalie and Traceleen represent nurturing, caring, and understanding. Traceleen does not judge but loves, and it is love like hers that saves many of Gilchrist's characters. Her strength is that of endurance, and her endurance helps many of Gilchrist's women survive and free themselves.

As the voice of four of the stories in the "Crystal" section, Traceleen has the opportunity to undercut much of the southern belle debutante mythology that many of the characters cling to. She is unswerving in her devotion to Crystal Weiss, but that does not stop her from seeing what is happening to her employer. In the first story in the section, the Weisses are flying to Memphis so that Joey Weiss, Manny Weiss's brother, can marry the daughter of the richest man in Memphis. On the plane, Manny's wife, Crystal, flirts shamelessly with Owen, Joey's col-lege roommate, and Traceleen notes her behavior while still supporting her employer for her kindness to her. She sees in Crystal's flirting a desire to rid herself of the constraints of the uptown society into which she has married. Traceleen sees below the surface of Crystal's erratic behavior and understands the loneliness and despair that drive it. The maid is a perfect storyteller because she can sympathize with Crystal while uncovering the failure of the society that produced her.

Traceleen tells her story from the beginning, when "Crystal came to New Orleans as a bride" (*VOJ*, 214). She relates how Crystal, ever the crusader for the underdog, drives her brother Phelan's Mercedes-Benz automobile into the antelope pen to free the animals her brother has bought to construct a little bit of Africa in Texas. He wants to provide businessmen too busy to go on safari the opportunity to come to his ranch and shoot exotic beasts. Crystal, appalled by his schemes, tries to thwart them.

Like Nora Jane Whittington and like her own cousin, Rhoda Manning, Crystal challenges the world of power and tradition. Rhoda and Crystal have more at stake in society, but like Nora Jane, they have a streak of the anarchist in them. They will not let convention and superficial social traditions determine their behavior. Crystal won't accept the fact that her brother has hired the first black student to attend Ole Miss to be his chauffeur, nor will she accept the penning of wild animals to be slaughtered. Her romantic notions of justice and fairness cause her to value Traceleen in ways the maid has never been valued before, so that she is not just an employee but sort of a sister. Traceleen looks at her employer and admits that "some people in the world, seem like they're just meant to be more trouble than other people. Demand more, cause more trouble and cause more goodness too" (*VOJ*, 231). That goodness is what keeps Traceleen working for Crystal. Traceleen values the romantic vision Crystal has not let be destroyed by the world in which she lives, and that vision becomes, in many of Gilchrist's characters, the impulse of the artist.

One of those artists, Frank Alter, modeled after Gilchrist's good friend Frank Stanford, befriends Crystal's son, King Mallison. Frank gives King some understanding of his outsider status in uptown New Orleans. Alter's suicide illustrates just how divergent the elements of Gilchrist's New Orleans really are. King, unable to find a place in a home in which he is "the stepchild" (*VOJ*, 217), runs away after Alter's death because no one in the family appreciates the value of the friendship the poet and the boy had. His return is celebrated by Traceleen and Crystal, who are willing to accept him as he is. The men in his life only want to fit him into a mold they have prepared for him. It is only through the women in his world that he is allowed grief and individual personality.

Despite the rebellious twist that many of Gilchrist's stories take, and in spite of the calamities that are always on the verge of happening in relationships within the stories, "human connections are important to the author."[5] Gilchrist seeks, in her fiction, to find ways for characters to change themselves, and Crystal's son King is one who, through the women who love him and the poet who teaches him, is able to change and to grow into a man who values people, not their social status or their wealth. As Gilchrist comments in a *Publishers Weekly* interview, she struggles to help characters move from spoiled self-absorption to a position that helps them see the world of danger and challenge outside themselves (Smith, 46). King Mallison and Rhoda Manning are exemplary of such a shift. Rhoda moves from being a self-centered child and adolescent to being an adult who wants to know more of the world and who wants to change it.

Drunk with Love

Gilchrist's third collection of stories, *Drunk with Love,* was first published in 1986. The title is inspired by the poem "A Man Lost in Love," written by Ralph Adamo, a friend and coworker on several publication projects. Adamo, poet, editor of the *New Orleans Review,* and former poetry editor of *Barataria,* a New Orleans magazine for which Ellen Gilchrist served as an associate editor, was an important part of Gilchrist's working life in New Orleans. Their collaboration on *Barataria* and their mutual close friendship with Frank Stanford brought them together.

The epigram for the book is taken from Albert Einstein and highlights what Gilchrist has been striving to capture in all her short stories: "What has been overlooked is the irrational, the inconsistent, the droll, even the insane, which nature, inexhaustibly operative, implants in an individual, seemingly for her own amusement."[6]

That sense of the unpredictable is introduced in the title story, which takes place in the same period of time as the story "Double Happiness Bun" published in *Victory over Japan.* "Double Happiness Bun" is told from Nora Jane Whittington's perspective, and the reader observes an earthquake in California and Nora Jane's response to it. In "Drunk with Love," Gilchrist takes her readers across San Francisco to Freddy Harwood's bookstore. He has just left Nora Jane and is trying to come to terms with her pregnancy and the possibility that the child is not his. At that moment, he experiences the same earthquake that Gilchrist describes in the earlier story. Nora Jane's experience of the earthquake is quite different from Freddy's. He experiences the first shocks, rushes to get all his customers out of the bookstore, and then calmly walks into the Vietnamese restaurant across the street to rescue two children from the burning building. However, he feels he cannot save his relationship with Nora Jane Whittington, nor can he, despite his heroism, get her to promise to marry him.

As in the other Whittington stories, Nora Jane is a free spirit. Her sense of what she wants can be found only in Sandy, the young man for whom she robbed Jody's Bar, fled to San Francisco, and left behind all that the mesdames of the Sacred Heart had tried to teach her. Freddy, for all his wealth, cannot make Nora Jane be "in love" with him, nor can she respond to him by behaving consistently. She returns home one day to find a poem from Sandy in her mailbox and she immediately goes to him. She cannot resist the power of his words because "Sandy was one of the few young men left in the Western world who understood the power of written communications" (*DWL*, 18). His little poem draws her back to her memory of their love. In this reunion, Gilchrist hails the power of youth and of the free spirit that Freddy Harwood lacks. The children in Nora Jane's womb seem most certainly to be Sandy's because Sandy has the soul of the poet while Freddy, for all his romantic notions, really has the mind and heart of a businessman. However, things could change, and they do, in yet another series of stories in Gilchrist's collection *Light Can Be Both Wave and Particle.*

With the next three stories in *Drunk with Love,* Gilchrist returns to her character Rhoda Manning. Gilchrist draws her at the ages of 5, 13, and 19, and shows the development of her independent spirit and her entrapment in marriage. At age five, in "1941," Rhoda is willful, headstrong, and insistent on her point of view. She battles her older brother, Dudley, to be first in her parents' affections. In "The Expansion of the Universe," which takes place in 1949, Rhoda is 13, just entering puberty, and insistent, once again, on her view of the world and of love. In this story, she falls in love with Bob Rosen, a college student dying of cancer. It is he who helps her to become a writer and to channel her furious energy. His love is a stabilizing and maturing influence on the young Rhoda. Gilchrist depicts the relationship as based on intellectual compatibility, a side of Rhoda's character that she must develop to become a writer, so Bob is her mentor as well as the object of her adolescent passion.

Contrasted with Bob's mature influence on the young Rhoda is the overwhelming power of the possibility of sex; Leta Ainsley, a stock Gilchrist sophisticate who has lived in Japan and has "strange ideas" (*DWL,* 38) about male-female relations, tells Rhoda about her "dryfucking" and offers to tell Rhoda all about sex. Rhoda's own personal anxiety over sex and love is heightened by the fact that her father moves the family once more; now Rhoda will have to go to a new school, will lose her position on the school newspaper, and will miss the class play. This move takes her away from Bob Rosen and once again forces her to look into herself to find out who she really is. Rhoda's mother, a southern belle, has no wisdom to offer because, as Rhoda points out, "you lived in the same house every day of your life. Your house is still there. Your mother is still there in that same house. You went to one school. You had the same friends" (*DWL,* 55). The stable world of Rhoda's mother is both the cause of her inability to understand her daughter and the reason her daughter feels no real bond with her. Rhoda is growing up in a new and changing world, and no one from the more settled previous generation has experience that can help.

The last Rhoda story in the collection, "Adoration," pictures Rhoda at 19, just married and pregnant. "She had made love to a boy one night after a fraternity party. The next week they ran away and got married. A month later she was living in a garage apartment in Atlanta putting him through school. Sex had been a big surprise to Rhoda. She had felt its mighty hand" (*DWL,* 58). Rhoda, once again into discovery and self-expression, tries to reconcile herself to her new husband and new life, but her spirit always refuses to be subdued. She, as the mother of two young children, is just as exuberant and self-willed as she was at age five.

Whereas some of the stories in *Drunk with Love,* such as "The Emancipator" and "Memphis," herald one-time appearances of characters, Anna Hand reappears in "Anna, Part I." This appearance—a reminder of her cameo part as the writer whose book Lady Margaret Sarpie reviewed in Gilchrist's short story "Looking over Jordan" from *Victory over Japan*—is a part of a series of stories, novellas, and novels focusing on the Hands. Clearly Anna Hand is the matriarch of a dynasty that flowers, throughout several of Gilchrist's books, with wit, love, and a good deal of southern guilt. Anna Hand, like Rhoda, is often distracted from her life as a writer by the "jaws of love" (*DWL,* 221). She is also, like Rhoda, a feisty, independent spirit who challenges the conventions of the world in which she lives, and she turns her experiences into her art. Margaret Jones Bosterli has also noted that, in "Anna, Part I," Hand can "understand what has happened to her only by making order of it in her fiction."[7] Having allowed herself to become obsessed with a "freckled, redheaded baby doctor" (*DWL,* 226) who is married and who has no intention of leaving his wife, Anna Hand finally sits down to write. The stories she writes "will tell [her] what is going on" (*DWL,* 238). "She takes control of her life by climbing out of bed and beginning to write. Her subject, of course, is what she knows best: the women's world, the love affair, and her survival" (Bosterli, 9).

Other characters who, in some way or another, take control of their lives are Traceleen and Crystal Weiss. In "Traceleen at Dawn," Gilchrist once again uses the black maid as the narrator and as the mediator between Crystal and her husband and Crystal and the world. Crystal takes control of her life by giving up alcohol, and Traceleen takes control of hers by being the voice that determines who gets a hearing. As the maid in an upper-class New Orleans household, she is privy to all the secrets that the rich hide from the world. Her employers, however, hide hardly anything at all. They fight over all manner of domestic and public issues: whether a three-year-old child will get into the exclusive Newman school without rigorous preschool training, whether Crystal should become absorbed in social causes to the exclusion of her husband, whether their son should get a haircut. Traceleen gathers it all in and feeds it back to the reader spiced with her wealth of wit and common sense. When Traceleen's husband, Mark, tells her not to worry about her employers, Traceleen asks, "How was I to stop? If you are with someone you begin to love them, you hear their joys and sorrows, you share your heart. That is what it means to be a human being. There is no escaping this" (*DWL,* 216). It is the humanity of Traceleen that, like Faulkner's Dilsey, saves the Weisses or at least saves Crystal and her children. It is the black woman's ability to remind her employer of what it means to be human that saves the story from being a shallow satire of upper-class southern life.

Two stories in the collection, "The Emancipator" and "Memphis," deal with the murder of young women by their husbands. In "The Emancipator," the unlucky Mae Lauer-Cheene returns from the Peace Corps and marries Hadi Karami Deeb so he won't lose his visa and be sent back to Lebanon. After the marriage, Hadi tries to control every aspect of Mae's life, and when she does not fit his expectations of a submissive wife, he beats her to death. In the second story, a young black man named Franke Brown marries Baby Kate Wheeler, the daughter of a long line of southern belles. Her father, Hailey, a poet and teacher who lives in his books, refuses to rescue his daughter when his sister tells him that Franke is beating her: " 'She has made her bed,' he said. ' I'm done with it. Done with her' " (*DWL*, 102).

Whether Gilchrist succeeds in articulating the nature of racial tension and the depth of sexual hatred in these two stories is debatable. Wendy Lesser, in "Home Movies," a review written for the *New York Times* in 1986, comments that these stories "suffer gravely from the disturbing cliches" that abound about race and gender.[8] However, the stories do show how each group stereotypes the other: whites stereotype blacks just as blacks stereotype whites, and men stereotype women just as women stereotype men. This refusal to see and respect the value of the other is what causes the violence. The depth of that violence falls on the two young women because, as Gilchrist sees it, they have most challenged the stereotypes of what women should be and thus disturbed the order of the way the world is supposed to work.

Light Can Be Both Wave and Particle

Light Can Be Both Wave and Particle, published in 1989, is Gilchrist's fourth collection of short stories, and is, by general critical estimation, the most uneven of her collections. The stories range from a long novella featuring Rhoda Manning at age 53 to a short, alternative ending to Gilchrist's novel *The Annunciation*. Once again, Gilchrist depends on characters who challenge the eternal verities of a shallow society, look for meaning in their lives in out-of-the-way situations, and affirm their own belief in the primacy of personal experience and love. In addition, several of the stories contain gems of Gilchrist wit and insight and introduce sparkling new characters.

The Rhoda stories frame the volume, which begins with two pieces featuring Rhoda's childhood and ends with the long story "Mexico." Rhoda's personality, firmly etched in earlier collections, might well be described with a line from "The Tree Fort." Of herself she says, "It never occurred to me to stop doing something just because someone was looking at me."[9] Although Rhoda has a finely tuned sense of herself, that sense is undercut by her gender. She wonders about her brother Dudley, "Why did they like him so much? Why was he so good? Why did he always get away with murder? Why did he have all the friends?" (*WP,* 19). Those questions echo throughout the story and throughout Rhoda's life. Being a woman can be a disadvantage in life, and although Rhoda fights it constantly, she has very few role models to give her strength. Her mother, again, is completely hopeless, apologizing for her inadequacies but showing Rhoda only that to be a woman is to be a failure. Her mother laments, "I'm so sorry. So sorry about everything. I'm doing all I can. I'm doing everything I know how to do" (*WP,* 23). Once again, the southern mother is ill-equipped to help her daughter weather the new world.

Two other stories, "The Time Capsule" and "Some Blue Hills at Sundown," also feature Rhoda; the first, as a small girl, and the second, as an adolescent learning about the sadness of love. In the second story, Gilchrist captures the adolescent girl's sense of loss. "It was the last time Rhoda would ever see Bob Rosen in her life" (*WP,* 26), and she will remember this moment, his "standing outside on the street, leaning against the building, smoking a cigarette and waiting" (*WP,* 27), for the rest of her life. Of course, she wants him to make love to her: "you said you'd do it to me. You promised me. You swore you would" (*WP,* 28). But Bob, understanding Rhoda's fury to live and seeing her vulnerability, won't "deflower" her. Instead, he admits, "I want you to know that I would have made love to you if I had been well. If you had been older and I had been well and things had been different. You are a wonderful girl, Rhoda" (*WP,* 30). So they part, and Bob Rosen "was counting the months he might live" (*WP,* 30).

At the end of the collection, Gilchrist inserts a long Rhoda story that calls attention, once again, to the character's search for self. Roy Hoffman calls this an inversion of a Hemingway story.[10] The macho explorer becomes the injured woman; Rhoda has sprained her ankle on a trip to a safari park while traveling in Mexico with her brother and her cousin. This story recalls the first Rhoda story, "Revenge," when Rhoda, Dudley, and St. John fought about who could use the broad jump pit. It has been a long time since Rhoda plotted her revenge against the men in her life who refused to let her prepare for the great Olympic event. Now she is rich and bored and owes the Internal Revenue Service 24 thousand dollars. She wants to escape, to remember the good things about her family. Reminiscing with Dudley and St. John, she tells the Mexican woman who is taking them to see a bullfight, "We used to stay all summer at our grandmother's house, Mariana. We had a wild time. I guess those summers were the best times of my life. There were all these children there. Because of that I always thought a big family must be a wonderful thing" (*WP,* 163). The nostalgia for the past, the acceptance of her family, and the closeness to her brother and her cousin give Rhoda a sense of fulfillment. She is even able to accept her cousin Anna Hand's suicide, calling it a good death.

However, the sense of order in the afternoon is shattered at the bullfight when Rhoda agrees to meet a matador at his hotel. Both Dudley and St. John order her not to go, but Rhoda responds, "I want to go and fuck this guy. I'm fifty-three years old. It's none of anybody's business. I don't mess around with your sex lives" (*WP,* 179). Once again, Rhoda must assert her identity, her right to act as she pleases. It is almost as if she were back at the broad jump pit, a girl not allowed to train with her brothers and male cousins for the Olympics, a girl confined to a bridesmaid's dress, a girl longing to be free.

If sex is what makes men free, then sex is what Rhoda will use, as she has been doing all along, to find her freedom. The matador offers that possibility, but Rhoda misses the opportunity; the whole trip to Mexico ends disastrously when Rhoda sprains her ankle.

Safe at home, she writes St. John, "Life is not easy for anyone. . . . We need something to hold on to in the dark and someone to remind us of where we really are. We are spinning in space on this tenuous planet. I won't let you forget that if you won't let me" (*WP,* 204).

Two additional characters from Gilchrist's other story collections reappear here in *Light Can Be Both Wave and Particle.* In "The Starlight Express," Nora Jane, deserted once again by Sandy, is on her way to Freddy when her twins are born prematurely. In "Traceleen Turns East," Traceleen, still Crystal Weiss's keeper and maid, reappears to chronicle yet another tale of Crystal and her exploits. This time, however, Traceleen participates fully when a robber with a 75-year-old kidnap victim appears at the Weiss's Story Street house. The kidnapper-robber ties up Crystal; the secretary, Bitsy Schlesinger (really a tennis partner of Crystal's); and Traceleen; then he waits for the kidnapee's husband to return to work, so he can call him and demand a million dollars for the return of his wife.

It is the voice of Traceleen that focuses and directs the story, and it is her perception of events and their meaning that makes the story amusing and a little satiric. She observes, "It is every person's duty to be prepared. . . . Just because we have faced one challenge doesn't mean there won't be another" (*WP,* 129). Her naive assessment of how yoga has prepared her for the role she plays in subduing the kidnapper and her continued commitment to doing yoga with Crystal for two hours every Tuesday and Thursday undercut the whole ethos of Crystal's fads and fetishes.

Two stories in the collection offer glosses and alternatives to the ending of *The Annunciation,* Gilchrist's first novel, published in 1983. The first story, "The Song of Songs," reunites Amanda McCamey with the daughter she gave up years ago for adoption, and the second story changes the ending of the book so that Amanda's young lover and the father of her newborn child does not die in the crash that sends his car careening off the highway. At the end of *The Annunciation,* the reader assumed that Will died as his child was being born, but in a postmodern postscript, Gilchrist brings him back to life and reunites him with Amanda and his child. These two stories strengthen the perception that Gilchrist sees her characters as developing far beyond the confines of the story.

Rhoda, Crystal, Nora Jane, Traceleen, Anna Hand, and others appear again and again, as if they were living their lives expecting Gilchrist to chronicle their exploits. This habit of tying her stories and her characters together, along with the stylistic device of letting her characters speak for themselves without editing or censoring, gives the stories a verisimilitude and reveals the limits of the narrator's knowledge without linking that limitation to Gilchrist herself. This technique allows Gilchrist to undercut the very traditions upheld by characters such as Rhoda's mother, Ariane, who desperately clings to the imagined southern way of life and tries without success to get Rhoda to accept it as well. But why should Rhoda accept such powerlessness? Her mother is never successful, and her father eventually leaves the family while the mother escapes back into the mythology of the southern belle.

Age of Miracles

Southern belles are satirized by Rhoda herself in Gilchrist's next book of short stories, *The Age of Miracles,* published in 1995. In "A Statue of Aphrodite," Rhoda, moving rapidly into middle age, has returned to live in Jackson, Mississippi, with her mother, the belle Ariane, and her father, the now impotent Dudley Sr. She is lured into Atlanta society by Dr. Carter Brevard, who sends her Laura Ashley dresses in sizes that do not even approximate Rhoda's figure and who asks her to be his hostess at the wedding of his daughter. Rhoda is able to laugh at her own behavior during the episode, which costs her almost 10 thousand dollars for clothes and plane tickets. She is also able to assess the vacuity of Atlanta society and the hopelessness of middle-aged passion, so she returns home, her fantasies of "getting laid" put to rest for the time being.

Rhoda appears again in several other stories in the collection. In fact, seven of the stories in the collection feature Rhoda Manning at some stage in her life, and another one is told about her from the point of view of her youngest son, Teddy. In "The Stucco House," the destructive power of Rhoda's quest for freedom and identity becomes clear when she accuses her husband Eric of trying to kill her. Her self-absorption, seen through the eyes of her seven-year-old son Teddy, is both a criticism of the adult world that has absolute power over children and a caution to adults to protect the greatest treasure they possess, their offspring.

The Rhoda stories do not look back to Rhoda as a child, but one, "Love of My Life," contains the hysteria of Rhoda in her 20s. She dreams that the thing she wants will show up, but neither Gilchrist nor Rhoda clarifies exactly what that thing is. Rhoda admits, "I have been waiting since I was fourteen years old for the thing I want" (*AM,* 217). In these stories, Rhoda is clearly the same feisty person she was when she set out to do the broad jump back in 1944. Although she has aged, had children, divorced, and remarried, her essential view of life has remained the same. "She is powerful and she wins" (*R,* viii).

Gilchrist deepens the relationship among her characters in all the stories in *Age of Miracles*. For example, in "The Raintree Street Bar and Washerteria," Sandy George Wade, Nora Jane Whittington's future boyfriend, is seen as a young man before he has met Nora Jane. Returning to New Orleans from a reform school in Texas, Sandy stops at the bar where all the New Orleans poets hang out. He is in search of Frank Alter, the poet who taught him poetry in reform school; he arrives only to find that Frank has just committed suicide, but the poems Sandy writes to Nora Jane years later in San Francisco now have a context and a beginning. He is, as Nora Jane has described him, a poet, a romantic figure. In addition, Frank is the same poet who befriended King Mallison, Crystal Weiss's son, and whose death has driven King to drugs and alcohol. Later, in "Among the Mourners," the head of the English Department at the University of Arkansas has to prepare the funeral for the poet. In another story, "Going to Join the Poets," Rhoda meets the head of the English department as she prepares to enter the creative writing program and work with Frank Alter, who will later commit suicide. Although not chronologically ordered, the stories link characters from different places and with different lives together, and in many ways, the stories come back to Rhoda.

Nora Jane Whittington also makes an appearance in "The Blue House." At 14, she picks mirlitons, a staple of the local diet, to sell to Langenstein's, "the richest grocery store in New Orleans, perhaps the richest grocery store in the world" (*AM*, 131), and she prays that her classmates at the Academy of the Sacred Heart will not see her. "She was the only girl at Sacred Heart so poor she had to sell vegetables to Langenstein's" (*AM*, 128). But she will achieve more than all her classmates at Sacred Heart because she has the "curiosity, and intelligence, [and] divine cynicism" (*R*, ix) of Rhoda. She is funny and sad; like Rhoda, she is a survivor.

Three stories that enrich the collection by developing new characters are "Love at the Center," "Joyce," and "Death Comes to a Hero." The narrator of the first story, a former "reporter for the *Times Picayune* in New Orleans" (*AM*, 149), tells the story with much of the vivacity of Rhoda looking for some new and interesting love affair, but Gilchrist distinguishes her from Rhoda by making her a taller version of that character and a lesbian who has given up women and married a stockbroker (*AM*, 149). She is in a perfect position to observe the love affair blossoming at the Washington Regional Medical Center for Exercise in Fayetteville, Arkansas. She and a retired English professor, Dr. Wheeler, comment on the relationship between the beautiful black-haired nurse, Athena Magni, and Andy Buchanan, a man who works at the center.

Gilchrist connects "Love at the Center" with other stories and characters in the collection through Dr. Wheeler, who used to teach English at the University of Arkansas, Fayetteville, and who taught Rhoda Manning during a seminar on James Joyce. Dr. Wheeler's observations about the Irish writer James Joyce in Gilchrist's story "Joyce" are reflected back to the young couple in "Love at the Center," and Rhoda's affair with Ketch McSweeney in "Joyce" is seen as a tawdry parody of the fresh young love of Andy for Athena, so lovingly described in "Love at the Center."

Gilchrist makes the contrast by placing "Love at the Center" and "Joyce" next to each other in the volume, so the good fortune that befalls Athena is contrasted with what is happening to Rhoda. Athena inherits four million dollars in a Cinderella ending, and she goes off to Paris and Italy with the blessing of Rosa Neely Parker, the 102-year-old woman who has left her the money. All the people at the center wish her well and hope that she will have a long and happy life. Andy Buchanan is bereft and the Center seems duller after Athena leaves, but that will change because "he's like a moon that's good at reflecting light. Sooner or later someone will be coming in that door to illuminate his face" (*AM,* 158). In contrast, Rhoda's lover, envious that the story she has written has been accepted by an important magazine, is frankly happy that she is returning to New Orleans to deal with her demanding husband and troublesome 16-year-old son. Ketch, unlike Andy, cannot bask in reflected glory.

Dr. Wheeler is also central to "Death Comes to a Hero," and his presence links the three stories in a way that gives all of them a sense of continuity and connectedness. The stories, positioned as they are in the center of *The Age of Miracles,* ground the book in Fayetteville, so that all the characters seem to pass each other on the streets of that small community. Once again, much of the story takes place at the Center for Exercise, but this time, Dr. Wheeler speaks with Brenda, a vivacious young woman who "only weighed two pounds more than when she had been Homecoming Queen of Fayetteville High" (*AM,* 171). Dr. Wheeler, the Joyce scholar, feels that he and Brenda are like Molly and Leopold Bloom from Joyce's novel *Ulysses.* Dr. Wheeler's growing fondness for Brenda is both paternal and sexual, as Leopold's was for Molly. Dr. Wheeler wishes to order Brenda's life by helping her apply for admission to the French department at the university. He sees himself as Leopold Bloom, who "would create order from chaos. Would create order from Molly, who knows no order" (*AM,* 177). Unfortunately, he dies before he can effect a change in Brenda's life. Gilchrist sees Dr. Wheeler as "a man who had outgrown evil. Who had never stopped to have an unkind thought" (*AM,* 184), so his death is indeed the death of a hero. The Dr. Wheeler stories illuminate the heart of *The Age of Miracles* in a way that brings freshness and joy to the book.

Rhoda: A Life in Stories

In 1995, Gilchrist collected all the Rhoda stories and published them along with excerpts from *Net of Jewels,* a novel about Rhoda Manning, in a book that gives a fuller picture of the character who has been central to much of Gilchrist's fiction. Taken together, the stories follow Rhoda Manning from the first story, "Revenge," depicting the willful child very much as Gilchrist saw herself as a child. She said in the introduction to the book that she remembered an incident in her own childhood involving "the famous Broad Jump Pit to which I was going to be denied

access" (R, vii). From that segregation from the sport of her brothers
came the character of Rhoda, a character who is "passion, energy, light"
(R, viii). That passion and energy grew as other stories took hold.
Gilchrist notes about Rhoda: "I have written many stories about Rhoda.
Some of them are blatantly autobiographical and some are made up.
Many are true to the real essence of the Rhoda I created on that fall
morning [the day she wrote "Revenge"]. Others miss the mark" (R, viii).
The process of writing about Rhoda, however, is important to Gilchrist's
craft. As she says of her Rhoda stories, and by extension, of her fiction,
"No writer truly understands the relationship between reality and storytelling. No real storyteller gives a damn about it except in retrospect or
in those rare generous moments when they think what they know can
be explained" (R, ix).

So Rhoda developed, the name borrowed from a friend out for an
afternoon run in Audubon Park. The stories are taken from Gilchrist's
childhood or from her imagination, but all the stories collected in *Rhoda:
A Life in Stories* add up to a character who is larger than the one in any
single story. Rhoda has become a hallmark of the woman who is willing
to fight all the silliness and vacuity of the Old South. If fighting means
leaving her husband, having affairs, going off to meet the poets, Rhoda
will try any of them because death is staying at home accepting what
her mother accepted. Robert Olen Butler has said that "Rhoda's feisty,
sexy, and devastatingly acute sensibilities make her one of the most
engaging and surprisingly lovable characters in modern fiction."[11] If she
is not exactly the most lovable, she is certainly the most voluble. Her
views on everything from marriage to the atomic bomb are insistent and
powerful, creative and destructive. She is also a life force, a survivor who
will not allow the loss of the love of her life to consume her; she is a
character who finally learns to tell "the truth" (R, 226).

Rhoda Manning, Crystal Manning Weiss, Anna Hand, Nora Jane
Whittington, Traceleen—all appear and reappear throughout Gilchrist's volumes of short stories. Although they come from different
walks of life, they represent for Gilchrist women who take charge of
their lives and who, at moments of particular clarity, can criticize themselves as well as the world they live in. Rhoda and Crystal break out of
the confining uptown New Orleans society to find lives for themselves,
even if, as in Crystal's case, that freedom is only temporary. Nora Jane
makes her own life from her imaginative response to reality, and she creates an almost utopian world for the children she bears. Anna Hand
makes light and truth by writing, even when her family doesn't want

her to, and finally, Traceleen watches and observes, but she also makes decisions about her life and refuses to accept a role that would denigrate her sense of herself and her sense of the women she loves and serves. All these voices grow stronger and stronger as Gilchrist accepts the power of her characters in her own writing. They take on a life of their own and insist, as Gilchrist observes in a *Publishers Weekly* interview, on "a role whenever I think of a new dramatic situation" (Smith, 46). Indeed, as Gilchrist observes in that same interview, "Human connections are important. . . . I think that in order to serve the vision I currently have of reality, I'm going to have to have at least five or six characters inter-playing" (Smith, 46). So the characters merge in the stories, meet each other outside the stories, and return in the novels to complete both their business and Gilchrist's business of finding a way to live in the world with truth and honor.

The Courts of Love

Published late in 1996, *The Courts of Love* returns to several characters seen in Gilchrist's earlier works. Nora Jane Whittington, who appears in almost every collection of Gilchrist's short stories, is central to the section entitled "Nora Jane and Company." In the nine stories that con-stitute this section, Gilchrist observes Nora Jane's life with Freddy Har-wood, the father, it is revealed, of only one of her twins, and the owner of Clara Books. He also has a trust fund, so Nora Jane has become rich in the 10 years since the birth of the twins, Tammili and Lydia. In becoming wealthy, Nora Jane could easily become dissatisfied, as do many of Gilchrist's women characters who are forced to live off their husbands' money. But she does not. In fact, Gilchrist seems to be striv-ing to show a happy marriage, to illustrate how people can, if they try, become close and loving. Having freed herself from the constraints of marriage and having found a source of income for herself in her writing, Gilchrist seems to want her favorite characters to have more charmed and charming lives than did the struggling Amanda McCamey or Rhoda Manning.

In the first story, "Perhaps a Miracle," Nora Jane wants to go back to school. At first, the discussion appears to follow the standard Gilchrist male-female conflict. Freddy whines, "How can I let you go to college? Every man at Berkeley will fall in love with you."[12] But soon it becomes clear that Freddy is fearful not because of his desire for ownership but because of his deep and abiding commitment to his wife and the twins.

His solution is to go back to school with her for a short time to renew
his acquaintance with Berkeley and to help her adjust. Freddy and his
friend Nieman Gluck both enroll, intending to drop out after Nora Jane
gets her bearings

Freddy's love is confirmed by his total commitment to the girls: "he
had delivered the twin baby girls who were his daughters. With no
knowledge of how to do it and nothing to guide him but love, he had
kept them all alive until help came" (*CL,* 5). He knew that Nora Jane
had another lover, and he sees, from the girls themselves, that only one,
Tammili, can possibly be his, but he follows his creed, to love that which
Nora Jane loves, and loves them both because they are both Nora
Jane's.

Lydia, the second twin, is, indeed, the daughter of Sandy George
Wade, the young man for whom Nora Jane turned bar thief, left New
Orleans, and came to California. Sandy has not been seen since before
the birth of the twins, but he too, returns for a brief appearance in *The
Courts of Love.* The mother of his current lover, Claudine, lives next door
to the Harwoods, and when Claudine brings her son to stay with her
mother, the little boy Zandia almost drowns in the Harwoods' pool.
Nora Jane's intuition that something is wrong draws her to the pool in
time to save the boy. When Claudine and Sandy George Wade come to
pick up Zandia from his grandmother's, Nora Jane worries that Sandy
will see her, or more troubling, see Lydia and want to claim her. Nora
Jane, terrified that her family will be pulled apart, asks Freddy to take
them away. They leave, and in typical fairy-tale fashion, find a charming
run-down mansion on the beach, buy it, and make plans for the permanent move.

Were it not for Gilchrist's ability to balance the fantasy of a perfect
life with the reality of suffering, the stories might seem cloying; however, the real world intrudes in many ways into the lives of Gilchrist's
characters, forcing them to reassess and to never forget to appreciate
their good fortune. In a story entitled "On the Problem of Turbulence,"
a friend of Freddy Harwood's, Sebranek Conrad, a prominent editor,
brings his lover, the writer Adrien Searle, to a book signing at Freddy's
bookstore. While they are in San Francisco, Sebranek hopes for a reconciliation with his son, and he hopes to convince Adrien to marry him.
However, fate in the form of a Muslim terrorist intervenes and Adrien is
murdered.

Violent incidents such as Adrien's murder occur randomly throughout the book, reminding the reader how fragile happiness really is. In

one story, a husband and wife lose their only child in a bombing at a day-care center she had been attending for only a week. In another story, Freddy Harwood, on a camping trip with his daughters, falls, and were it not for the twins' quick thinking, Nora Jane's intuition, and the sharp eyes of a forest ranger, he would have died as well. These random incidents sharpen Gilchrist's appetite for joy.

Happy families may be a hedge against the damage the world can do to the individual, but Nora Jane remembers her unhappy family. The death of Adrien Searle reminds her of her own childhood: "This was like her childhood had been, fear and anger and uncertainty. Evil that seemed to come from nowhere and darken the sun. One moment her mother would be sober and trying to get in good with her. The next moment she was crying and begging for help and saying she was going to die" (*CL*, 62). Those moments of terror, when Nora Jane would run to her grandmother's house on Webster Street, are hidden in her past, but the catastrophe of Adrien's death reminds her of the fragility of her happiness and the power of evil to destroy her life and her children's lives.

That New Orleans past also returns in the face of a police officer investigating the murder. Jason Hebert is from Louisiana, and as Nora Jane looks at him, the terror of her past returns: "Nora Jane looked up and met those eyes again, extraordinary eyes. The eyes of an altar boy, a darkened church on Poydras or Melpomene. Incense, the mass being read in Latin, death and the smell of death" (*CL*, 61). In the character of Jason Hebert, Gilchrist captures, once again, the power of the old southern city, the possibility of evil, and the presence of death. In the few lines describing the transplanted police officer, Gilchrist also recaptures her most powerful image of place.

The stories in *The Courts of Love* contain a determination to find and keep love and to create the happy families that many of the characters did not have as children. Gilchrist interweaves the lives of characters from story to story, so that most of the major characters are connected in one way or another. Freddy's friend, Neiman Gluck, falls in love with Stella Light, a biologist at Berkeley. She is the cousin of the couple whose child has been killed in the day-care center bombing. The couple come, with their two foster girls, to Neiman's wedding at the Harwoods' new house on the ocean, and so Gilchrist is able to make family and friendship connections among a large, extended group of people. This loving group replaces the repressive southern families that Rhoda and Amanda McCamey grew up in. It is not simply blood but love that links people, and the relationships are not destructive but creative.

Another young girl, Aurora Harris, so typical of Gilchrist's early fiction, appears to remind readers of Rhoda Manning as a child. Nora Jane might have traded her romantic dream for a comfortable reality, and her twins are too well loved to rebel, but Aurora must struggle to find her place in the world. She appeared in one story in *The Age of Miracles,* "Among the Mourners," the story of Frank Alter's funeral. This young girl is connected by the death of the poet to a host of other Gilchrist stories and characters, and her desire for a voice is reminiscent of the struggles of all Gilchrist's artists. In *The Courts of Love,* Gilchrist strengthens Aurora's voice. She has the temperament of Rhoda Manning. Everything affects her deeply. When she fails to make the cheerleading squad in junior high school, her comment has all the rich hyperbole of some of Rhoda's pronouncements: "There is nothing left to do but go on and try to get into medical school and go to Zaire and try to save some kids from dying of Ebola" (*CL,* 236). In addition, Aurora, like Rhoda, has the ability to see early that she must escape her family: "Anything to escape the middle-class values my mother is espousing in order to save herself from worrying about the real fear and terror of every living human being, which is death and decay" (*CL,* 246).

Like Gilchrist's other fiction, *The Courts of Love* is incremental; stories build on earlier stories, characters return from earlier works, and incidents are reminiscent of the earlier happenings. Gilchrist, in her effort to make meaningful connections, links her characters and her books in ways that enrich both the old and the new ones; undoubtedly, readers will see a good deal more of those characters who appear here only briefly, as they insist later on their own hour on center stage.

Chapter Four

Novels of Personal Growth

The Annunciation and *Net of Jewels*

The phenomenal success of Ellen Gilchrist's first book of short stories, *In the Land of Dreamy Dreams,* heralded a new voice in the southern short story, but Gilchrist did not immediately follow that collection with another. Instead, she published *The Annunciation,* a woman's bildungsroman about the life of Amanda McCamey, "a pretty girl. Prettiest girl in Issaquena County. And from good stock."[1] In this work, Gilchrist's method of storytelling expands beyond the bounds of the short story and develops a generational style. The web of connections (between people and across time) that Gilchrist spins in the unwritten space between related short stories becomes the explicit structure of the novels, and that method and structure give the novels a sense of participating in a history and in families that exist, as the characters in the short stories do, outside the pages of the book.

Several other novels followed *The Annunciation.* In 1988, *The Anna Papers* appeared, featuring the writer Anna Hand, who bore the brunt of Lady Margaret Sarpie's vacuous criticism in the earlier short story "Looking over Jordan." Anna Hand, the successful writer, is the titular matriarch of a clan that looks to her for guidance and that sees in her talent the flourishing of the creative urge of the family. She is the voice and critic of the family. In that way, though childless herself, she gives a sense of identity to her brothers, their children, and others connected with the group.

Next, Gilchrist brought together the Hands and the Mannings (Rhoda Manning's extended family) in a book of interrelated novellas, *I Cannot Get You Close Enough,* a book that chronicles the complicated relationships and interrelationships of the children and adults of the two clans. This book, more novel in its structure than short story, acts as a link between the short stories and the novels, sharing some features of both.

In the next novel, *Net of Jewels,* published in 1992, Gilchrist returns to Rhoda Manning to flesh out the rebellious child of the early short stories and to give her voice political and social depth and significance. Rhoda has the same spark she had as a willful young girl facing her brother and cousins, but she begins, in the novel, to see the political significance of her rebellion and to take some small steps toward responsibility for her longings and desires.

Starcarbon, published in 1994, continues Gilchrist's technique of taking minor characters from earlier books and giving them center stage so they have their own stories. The young woman, Olivia de Havilland Hand, brought to the Hand clan by Anna from her Cherokee mother's reservation in Oklahoma, decides that she must know not only her father's family but her mother's as well, if she is going to know herself. Her journey back to her Cherokee Indian past in Oklahoma, her search for her roots, and her awareness of her place in the Hand clan helps her learn about herself and find her place in the larger world.

In *Anabasis,* discussed in chapter 1, Gilchrist journeys into the distant past to capture a story of love and freedom that is based on a tale she made up as a child. Even though Gilchrist moves away from the contemporary South to show a woman's liberation in ancient Greece, the story develops a thematic relationship to the other novels, for all are, on one level or another, quests for self-definition and freedom among women.

Ellen Gilchrist's novels divide themselves into two types: novels of personal growth, or bildungsroman, as seen in *The Annunciation* and *Net of Jewels,* and novels of dynasty and family development, illustrated by *The Anna Papers, I Cannot Get You Close Enough,* and *Starcarbon.* Both *The Annunciation* and *Net of Jewels,* and to a certain extent, *Anabasis,* are chronicles of young women searching for freedom and independence. Even though that search takes place within the context of extended families or communities that control and determine the destinies of the members, Amanda McCamey, Rhoda Manning, and the slave girl Auria struggle and, to a certain extent, succeed in creating a place for themselves in the world. Amanda's and Rhoda's struggles follow similar patterns and take place within the context of similar societies. The two characters, brought up during World War II, also have similar life experiences and as characters on journeys toward self-awareness and freedom, they develop along parallel lines.

The Annunciation

The Annunciation, published in 1983, opens with all the trappings of a southern dynastic novel. The young girl, Amanda McCamey, is brought home to Esperanza Plantation when her father, Leland McCamey, dies in World War II. Her mother, given over to grieving for her dead husband, leaves the child in the care of her cousin Guy and the family servants. Idyllic summer days swimming with Guy, four years her senior, eventually lead to her pregnancy and her exile to the city of New Orleans to have her baby. Yet her plantation past is a rock in the center of her memory. It is the home she longs for but eventually must escape if she is ever to have a life of her own.

Central to that past are her father, who was acquitted after he shot a crazy man who had come gunning for him; her great-grandmother, who outlived two husbands; and her grandmother, who ran the great house with energy—"these were the people of Esperanza Plantation. These were the people who taught Amanda everything she would always know" (*A*, 6). Her sense of herself is defined by the women who take her to New Orleans to have her baby, by the nuns who care for her while she is pregnant, and by the memory of Leland, her father. However, as much as these people give Amanda strength, they are the people whose values Amanda must reject in order to find herself and her voice.

After her baby girl is born and given up for adoption, Amanda is reclaimed by her mother and grandmother. She will be sent to Virginia Women's Seminary. She will have her old life back, as if she had never had the child. "Her grandmother had sold the Deadning, a 60-acre stand of wooded land, and put the money in an account for the next six years of Amanda's life. 'She will have her chance,' she told the rest of the family. 'She is all that we have left of Leland' " (*A*, 21).

However, the family's reclamation of her is contingent upon Amanda accepting the role of the southern belle. Her grandmother buys her new clothes, and she and Amanda's mother, along with Sister Celestine from the home for unwed mothers, put her on a train for Virginia. At first Amanda accepts the role, "settl[ing] back into the seat, making a catalogue in her mind of her treasures, imagining herself in her new white formal, surrounded by young men in uniform" (*A*, 23). That role soon palls, however, and Amanda finds herself straining against the bonds of propriety and compliance that the women in the family expect of her. "I don't know why I've been letting everyone boss me around. . . . No one can make me do anything I don't want to do" (*A*, 24).

As Charles Stubblefield notes in his review of *The Annunciation*, Amanda's mother and grandmother "are motivated to hide the shame and to build an elaborate lie to protect the family name."[2] And it is the necessity of seeing her life as shameful that Amanda, in the exuberance and innocence of youth, cannot accept. In defiance, she drinks champagne with a writer traveling on the train and offers to let him kiss her. If southern fiction is often based on the idea of romance, Amanda's meeting with the southern writer embodies that romantic notion. Gilchrist undercuts that tradition, however, when the writer, realizing how young Amanda really is, tells her with regret: "It's against the laws of the Commonwealth of Virginia for a man my age to kiss girls your age" (*A*, 29). Amanda, crushed, thinks her day is ruined, but the writer consoles her and cautions, "Don't let them make you forget who you are" (*A*, 29), a warning that it will take Amanda several years and much heartbreak to heed.

As *The Annunciation* develops, Amanda is forced to look at how the notion of romance has destroyed her sense of herself. First, at school after giving up the baby, she hates her body. Later, she hates other things about herself and the world in which she lives. Finally, she struggles to become free, but it is almost like cutting off a limb to extricate herself from the prison of life she has built up around herself.

Amanda's analogue character, Rhoda Manning as a young child, looked at the world of women in the Delta and vowed never to marry because marriage would prevent her from fulfilling her dream. She tells her grandmother, "I'm going to New York and be a lawyer and save people from the electric chair" (*DD*, 120). Amanda has the spunk and honesty of the young Rhoda, and even promises herself that she "will never marry anyone and I will never have [another] baby. . . . No one will ever make me do anything I don't want to do as long as I live" (*A*, 37). Gilchrist makes a further connection between the two by giving Rhoda's grandmother's maid, Baby Doll, the same name as the maid at Esperanza Plantation. It is as if the two characters, Rhoda and Amanda, are on some level one. Their pasts, the history of their families, are intertwined in the "thirteen feet of black topsoil" (*A*, 3) of the Delta they both rise from.

They grow from the same source, and they must both escape from that world in order to survive. Amanda's quest for survival meets many of the same obstacles as Rhoda's. Both marry young and have children, even though both swear, in order to remain free, that they will not marry. Amanda even imagines loving a young man with cancer much like Rhoda actually does during high school.

Gilchrist, in this first novel, is opposed to the traditional mores that bind women, and when Amanda goes to a gynecologist because of complications from the cesarean section she had at the birth of her daughter, the young doctor marvels at the misinformation that has been fed to her about pregnancy and birth. "Every stupid and pointless thing in the out-worn gothic mores of the Deep South was in the garbled story she was telling him" (*A, 39*). Gilchrist combines her own criticism of the "out-worn gothic mores of the Deep South" with sympathy for the young doctor trapped in the same world. Unlike Amanda, however, he isn't strong enough to fight the world in which he lives; instead, he anes-thetizes his pain with drugs. Gilchrist shows this as one escape, but not the one that leads to fulfillment and self-knowledge.

The Annunciation moves from crisis to crisis, forcing Amanda to make choices that will bind or free her. Gilchrist develops the action in this way to illustrate the strong pull of southern tradition that Amanda must fight against at every turn. When visiting her grandmother, Amanda is reminded of the powerful pull of her grandmother's person-ality and of the traditions she lives by. The old woman continues to insist that her granddaughter will never find peace in the life she has chosen: "You aren't going to find any peace until you accept the Lord as your savior" (*A, 51*). But Amanda, married to the Jew Malcolm Ashe, sees her grandmother's religion as shallow hypocrisy that grows out of the old woman's naive assumptions about people. Her grandmother also believes that Amanda was ignored by the Junior League in New Orleans because of her foul mouth, when ironically it was because she married a Jew. Amanda understands the subtle exclusions that the Junior League imposes on women who marry Jews. The narrow society of New Orleans, the empty rituals of her grandmother's generation, and her confining marriage to Malcolm Ashe all drive Amanda further and fur-ther from her goal of freedom.

It is not until her grandmother dies and she sees Guy again that Amanda can contemplate the kind of life she dreamed for herself. In fact, when she returns to New Orleans after her grandmother's funeral, she really hears for the first time the way her acquaintances converse. She asks herself, "What am I doing here? . . . What am I doing in a place where people hate each other? No, that's wrong. They hate them-selves. That's who they really hate" (*A, 69*). Ironically, of course, it is not only self-knowledge that comes with the death of her grandmother, the woman who has always held up the code of behavior before Amanda's eyes; it is also money. The old woman has "left [Amanda] half of Esper-anza Plantation, seven hundred acres of Delta land under cultivation" (*A, 94*), so her own money also gives Amanda the possibility of freedom.

Evidence of the self-hatred that Amanda experiences in the world of uptown New Orleans is further graphically depicted in a scene that she witnesses outside the ladies' room of a posh New Orleans restaurant. A woman and her husband are arguing about the woman's behavior. Apparently, she has objected to his inviting his mistress to be a part of the Comus Ball during Mardi Gras, and her husband is ordering her to return to his colleague's party and "act like a lady" (*A,* 75). If she won't swallow her pride and call his mistress to invite her to the ball, he will send her home to her mother and take their son away from her. The rage Amanda feels as she listens to the man imposing his southern mores on his wife even to the point of ordering her to "pick up [his mistress] and take her with you to the ball" (*A,* 76) drives her out of the restaurant. Meanwhile, the woman and her husband return to the party. That scene would offer only generalized significance as a critique of the patriarchal privilege of New Orleans except that the woman is Barrett Clare, the daughter Amanda gave up for adoption more than 30 years earlier. Although Amanda is not aware of their connection at the time of the incident, Gilchrist makes it clear that Barrett is trapped in the same hypocritical morass that her mother finds herself in.

Flight from New Orleans is Amanda's only escape from the stagnant society that expects her to behave in certain preconceived ways and that criticizes any deviation from strict social norms. Amanda cannot do it alone, but Gilchrist notes that "Amanda had an ally during the years she was married to Malcolm, a black woman named Lavertis" (*A,* 79). Although the character of Lavertis is not so fully developed as Traceleen, Crystal Manning Weiss's maid in several short stories and novellas, she has many of the same qualities. She helps Amanda stop drinking when all her social equals urge her to continue; further, she sees the good in Amanda and supports her when even Malcolm is frustrated and critical. Lavertis is able to show Amanda, just like Traceleen shows Crystal, that her own goals are valuable. Amanda has enrolled at Tulane University to get her degree in foreign languages, and Lavertis is the only one who says "I am so proud of you" (*A,* 91). Lavertis alone, however, cannot free Amanda and give her a sense of value; Amanda must take some steps herself.

Her first step is to write to Malcolm admitting, "I don't know what it is I'm looking for. I know it is wrong for me to take your love and life and use them as props" (*A,* 115). That letter begins to free her. Then, an opportunity to translate *The Lost Wedding Songs of Helene Renoir,* an eighteenth-century French poet "locked away with the sisters of Lyons for an illicit love affair" (*A,* 148), takes her to Fayetteville, Arkansas, where her true transformation begins. Finally, she has something to challenge her intellect and to focus her quest for freedom. Parallels abound between Amanda and the woman whose poems she studies. Helene has an illegitimate child that the nuns take away from her, just as two hundred years later the nuns take Amanda's child away from her. Helene is a poet, but she never really gets a chance to develop because after the child is born she is driven to suicide by her loneliness. Amanda, too, is a writer, and she must decide whether she will succumb, as Helene did, to the loneliness: "All my languages, all my gifts, all my words and still I am alone" (*A,* 295), she thinks. Will she be able to overcome the "remorse and loneliness" (*A,* 295)? Or will she, like Helene, end it all?

Free of New Orleans and engrossed in the only thing that has ever really mattered to her, Amanda begins to luxuriate in the freedom the university town of Fayetteville offers. She thinks, "I finally made it to the free people" (*A,* 151). But Amanda soon realizes that freedom can be very lonely, and when she meets a young guitarist named Will Lyons (whose last name connects him to the poet whose work Amanda is translating), she falls deeply in love. Despite her friend's admonition, "work is the thing that stays" (*A,* 202), Amanda realizes on one level that freedom without love is only loneliness, and she needs love to complete herself. Her body, ravaged by her first pregnancy almost 30 years earlier, cries out for love, and her mind, trapped in the rigid confines of the rules of translation, cries out to create, not simply translate, another woman's love. Amanda will not be truly herself until she resolves the conflict between work and love.

After a year in Fayetteville, Amanda is surer of herself, but the real loneliness in her life has still not been assuaged. There is still the ghost of the child in her past, the child she must find in order to be complete. Will recognizes that and suggests, "Maybe you ought to go on and find that girl, Amanda. Maybe you ought to put that behind you" (*A,* 230). Her cousin Guy has already hired someone to find his daughter and has secretly watched her play tennis, but Amanda still refuses to face her old grief. However, after Will leaves Fayetteville, Amanda finds out she is carrying his child, so she must make a decision about the first one, the girl in New Orleans.

Again the old alternation of grief and excitement emerges. Guy arrives and tries to get Amanda to go to New Orleans to meet their daughter, Barrett Clare, but Amanda refuses. The child inside her also makes its demands, and Amanda is torn between the fetus and her work. "It's no good, she thought. It's all wrong. It's a parasite. It's going to suck the life out of me" (*A,* 301). The old fear of losing herself comes

back with a vengeance with Guy's demand that she meet their daughter
and with the discovery of her new pregnancy. Yet Helene's suicide is not
the answer, nor is an abortion, and Amanda decides that she will be "the
oldest pregnant woman in Fayetteville" (*A*, 310).

That decision made, Amanda can truly begin to live her life. Her further decision that she will have the child alone, that she will not be
dependent on the father to help rear it, and that she will make it happy
follows swiftly on the first. "I am going to have this baby, and I am
going to make it happy" (*A*, 311). Her decision shifts the focus from
Amanda to the future she plans to live in. Her friend, Katie Vee, tells
everyone of Amanda's baby, "It doesn't have a father. She willed it into
being all by herself out of light and air. Well, I swear I think she's start-
ing to believe it" (*A*, 315). Thus the book title becomes clear. Amanda's
search for herself ends in her true independence, which is free of the men
who have disappointed and bored her, but which is also linked to life
through the child in her body. That independence becomes almost a
mantra in her mind. "I am in charge of my own life and the life of this
child. Nothing bad will happen because I will it so. My will be done,
goddammit. My will be done. . . . I will take back the territory of my
life. Now I will take back all the territory" (*A*, 325).

At 44, Amanda McCamey becomes her own person, and the boy,
born on Christmas day and named Noel, signals the new life she will
have. Also on Christmas, her colleague comes to tell her that her book
has been accepted, so she has almost reached fulfillment. Only the
daughter, lost in New Orleans, remains, and Amanda promises herself
that she will find her. "I'll go find her as soon as I'm well. . . . I'll get on
a plane and fly to New Orleans . . . and tell her what was done to me.
. . . I'll tell her what those goddamned nuns did to me and she will love
me" (*A*, 352).

If Amanda finds happiness and completion at the end of *The Annunciation*, Gilchrist has a problem with Will Lyons. What should she do with
the young man if his presence might lessen Amanda's independence?
That is certainly a concern because, when Will is there, Amanda is less
than completely focused on her work. Gilchrist solves the problem by
leaving the reader with the impression that Will is killed in an auto accident when he is on his way home to see his child and Amanda. *The
Annunciation* ends with his car careening off a mountain road. "The car
lifted off into the still white air, describing a long curve like a stone
thrown into a lake. Then it began its downward spiral. Then there was
nothing at all" (*A*, 352). Amanda is, unknowing, left at the end of the

novel to make her own future, and as she falls asleep she dreams, "my life on my terms, my daughter, my son. My life leading to my lands forever, and ever and ever" (*A,* 353).

Later, Gilchrist rethinks that ending. In a short story in the collection *Light Can Be Both Wave and Particle,* she articulates what she wants for the daughter and for Will, but for the first ending, it is clear that Gilchrist sees her protagonist's independence in terms of freedom from men who would define her. In *The Annunciation,* Amanda frees herself from her cousin and her husband, and fate frees her from Will.

Several of the themes of the early short stories find their way into Gilchrist's first novel. The pull of the Old South against the independent dreams of young women reiterates the clash between Rhoda and her mother in the early stories. The quest for freedom is realized in *The Annunciation* because this, her first novel, shows Amanda's life from early childhood to middle age. The progress of Amanda McCamey in this one text mirrors the progress that women like Rhoda make over several volumes of short stories. What Gilchrist succeeds in creating is an internal view of the female psyche (Thompson, 102). Amanda, like many of the protagonists of Gilchrist's short fiction and other novels, suffers throughout most of her life from what Jeanie Thompson and Anita Garner refer to as "an extended downhill slide" (Thompson, 102). She must stop that slide in order to develop a sense of herself. Like many southern women, she constantly encounters obstacles to self-definition and fulfillment. It is the struggle to overcome those obstacles that enriches Amanda's character and allows her, at the end of the novel, to proclaim her independence.

Net of Jewels

Although Amanda can declare her independence at the end of *The Annunciation,* the task is not so easy for another Gilchrist heroine. Rhoda Manning, the feisty young girl of much of Gilchrist's short fiction, finds herself on the cusp of womanhood trapped by her family, by her unfortunate marriage, and by her two demanding children. Her struggle to free herself and to define herself is not as successful as Amanda's because, at the novel's close, she is still caught in the net of family and social expectations; however, the novel does create possibilities that Rhoda will take advantage of later on.

Published in 1992, *Net of Jewels* focuses on five years in the young adult life of the character who is most closely autobiographical in her conception and realization. In Rhoda, Gilchrist has invested a good deal of her fictional energy, and the conflict in both the author and her character between the southern belle and the independent woman rages fiercely in every stage of the novel, just as it does in many of the short stories. *Net of Jewels* is Gilchrist's attempt to locate that conflict between Rhoda's character and that specific time in American history—the middle of the century, when women all over America began to ask themselves what life had to offer. It is also a time when the Supreme Court decision *Brown v. Board of Education* initiated the civil rights movement in the very part of the country where Rhoda comes to live.

The novel begins when Rhoda is in college, and the family decides to move to Dunleith, Alabama, near Aberdeen, where her father's family has made its fortune. Rhoda's father, Dudley Manning, has always controlled his children; he is, as Rhoda describes him, "a vain and beautiful man who thinks of his children as extensions of his personality" (*NJ,* 3). This is the man who has to be understood in order to understand Rhoda's struggle, and in *Net of Jewels,* Gilchrist sets out to piece together the puzzle of Rhoda's personality and the hold her father has on her. As Rhoda says, "You have to know that [her relationship with her father] to understand this story, which is about my setting forth to break the bonds he tied me with" (*NJ,* 3). The upheaval that breaking free entails is the core of the novel, and *Net of Jewels* is the most extended study Gilchrist has ever done of Rhoda. Her life, in kaleidoscopic images, is steadily revealed in the earlier short stories, but the short story form, because it does not provide depth of analysis, makes Gilchrist's pictures of Rhoda seem like snapshots. The novel allows Gilchrist the opportunity to examine Rhoda as she makes small steps towards independence, and it provides the opportunity to paint a portrait with all Rhoda's light and shadow.

The novel covers the period from the time Rhoda is 19 and her family returns to the South until the time she is 24, has just had an abortion, and is trying to free herself for the second time from Malcolm Martin, her husband and the father of her two sons. Those five years are critical in the life of Rhoda Manning and in the life of the nation, and Rhoda, during the course of the story, encounters the Ku Klux Klan, civil rights lawyers, and several examples of injustice to blacks that she will someday have to integrate into her picture of life if she is ever to become a serious person.

If it is Dudley Manning who dominates and controls the family, it is Ariane, her mother, who must turn Rhoda into an acceptable southern belle. Weak as she is in the face of Rhoda's fury, Ariane bends to her job of making her daughter a suitable jewel for her husband's diadem. The method used is to convince young girls that their bodies are ugly and then force them to focus on making their bodies pleasing to men while their minds stagnate. When Rhoda tells her mother, "I won the freshman writing contest," her mother replies, "You've gained so much weight. . . .We'll take you to a doctor tomorrow and get you some of the new pills" (*NJ*, 21). This exchange indicates the mother's desire to control her daughter's physical attractiveness at the expense of her mental development. Rhoda must constantly struggle with the woman who should be helping her free herself; instead, her mother aids her father in keeping her dependent and infantile. Rhoda dare not do battle with her father because he controls the purse strings that allow her the illusion of some small measure of freedom. Instead, she does what many young women do; she attacks her mother. Rhoda rages against her mother's acquiescence to the will of Dudley Manning; she lashes out at her mother to embarrass her in front of the community. "Shut up Mother," Rhoda tells her. "Please mind your own goddamn business" (*NJ*, 29). Of course, Ariane's only business is to control Rhoda so that her daughter will be a pleasing young woman who is a credit to the Manning family. Rhoda is, most certainly, Ariane's business.

Rhoda's mother has accepted her place in the patriarchal structure of the Old South and is intent on turning Rhoda into a compliant and infantile woman like herself. However, there are women in the novel who offer Rhoda models for a different life. Rhoda knows her world well enough to understand, "Anything I wanted I could have. All I had to do was stay on my diet and be 'nice to people' " (*NJ*, 30). However, it is almost impossible for her to do either, so she is attracted to people, especially women, who have found a way to negotiate the terrain of adulthood and have managed to grow up. Two of those women are Patricia Morgan and Derry Waters. Both have achieved wholeness in their lives and in their relationships, and Rhoda is attracted to them as surrogate mothers precisely because they offer maturity and independence, two qualities her own mother does not have.

Patricia Morgan, "an exotic woman" (*NJ*, 42) whom Rhoda meets at the country club pool, is perhaps the first woman that Rhoda has seen who has lived with and overcome a handicap. She has had polio and wears braces on both her legs. She is also from Massachusetts, and as Rhoda examines her attraction to Patricia Morgan, she realizes that "[Patricia Morgan] represented something I longed for, but barely knew existed, a world of rational thought, coolness, Puritan simplicity" (*NJ,* 42). There is in Patricia Morgan a possibility of a life for Rhoda that does not entail the destruction of her own will and personality, and the older woman urges Rhoda not to belittle herself. "Who told you," she asks Rhoda as they sit by the country club pool, "not to be proud of your accomplishments?" (*NJ,* 46). Rhoda can only answer, "Well, they mostly want me to stop being fat. It embarrasses them if I'm fat" (*NJ,* 46). Still trapped in the confining strictures of the southern belle, Rhoda can only long to have Patricia Morgan's coolness and rationality.

Perhaps the polio has freed Patricia Morgan; perhaps her northern education has. Regardless of what has freed her, Rhoda admires her courage and wants to learn from her. Unfortunately, that possibility is destroyed when Rhoda wrecks the car she is driving and kills Patricia's only child. The accident is doubly tragic because the Morgans' older son has already been killed, and the couple are now left childless in an alien society that cannot help them in their grief.

The guilt that Rhoda feels over the accident that killed Clay Morgan allows Dudley Manning to manipulate her into leaving Vanderbilt and going to the University of Alabama at Tuscaloosa. She observes, "So the con was on. He knew when to strike. Whether or not the accident had been my fault the guilt was mine and it was a vein anyone could mine for years. So of course Daddy was the first to get a pick and go to work on it" (*NJ,* 73). The metaphor of the vein is appropriate because Dudley Manning has made his wealth in mines, and he plunders his daughter's psyche as he plunders the earth. The accident and the move to Tuscaloosa prevent Rhoda from learning more about independence and self-worth from Patricia Morgan. With her transfer from Vanderbilt to the University of Alabama, yet another avenue of possible freedom and growth is closed to her. She is entering the world of the southern belle, and she is entering a time in her life when young women are most vulnerable to the need for physical love and affection.

At Alabama, Rhoda becomes involved in her sorority, meets a young man studying engineering at Georgia Tech, marries him, and quickly has two children. It certainly seems as if any chance of freedom has been traded for the possibility of a husband and a family, the conventional route for a young woman in the mid-fifties to take. Malcolm Martin is certainly a roadblock to Rhoda's notions of freedom. He wants her to be a conventional wife, to keep her mouth shut, to cook the dinner, and to care for the children. Her boredom at these tasks and her unwillingness to submit her personality to his create strife in the marriage from the very beginning. That conflict is already developed in several of the earlier short stories, as is some of the action of this period in the novel. What has not been previously characterized is Rhoda's friendship with Derry Waters. Derry is a cousin by marriage of Rhoda's close friend and confidant, Charles William Waters, and she has led an independent life. Once a reporter in Washington, D.C., who went to jail for her principles, she is, when Rhoda meets her, deeply involved in the Montgomery, Alabama, civil rights struggle. Immediately, Rhoda realizes that Derry, like Patricia Morgan, is special. "She was beautiful. And something more. Some kind of power I had never seen in a woman" (*NJ*, 244). Rhoda has already experienced the undercurrent of racial terror that the South hides. When she and Charles William go to the Klan meeting, she is terrified by the atmosphere of violence, but in Derry she sees someone strong enough to face the faceless hoods of the Klan and not be afraid, and it is that fearlessness and power that Rhoda envies and loves.

Of Derry, Rhoda observes, "Except for Patricia Morgan, she may have been the first truly grown woman I had ever known, a full and complete woman who was free to act" (*NJ*, 247–48). In contrast, Rhoda sees herself "as a half-baked, not dry behind the ears, slightly overweight, pretty much ruined forever person" (*NJ*, 248), and that difference plagues Rhoda and challenges her to be more than she is.

But still the men control her and pull her back. Her father and her husband manipulate her: After a brief separation during which she returns to her family in Dunleith, Rhoda goes back to Malcolm, and they move to Alexandria, Louisiana, where he has gotten a job as an engineer at the paper plant. Again, Rhoda finds herself in the unsatisfying role of wife and mother.

Related to Rhoda's dissatisfaction with herself and her world is her drinking. Her father and mother want her to stop, ostensibly so she can manage the children, but her children, as much as she loves them, bore her, and drink brings some excitement into her life. Of course, it also creates problems. She gets pregnant when she is drunk; she has an affair under the influence of alcohol; and she was almost certainly intoxicated when she crashed the car and killed Clay Morgan. But drink is also liberating. As Rhoda tells her doctor, "I only drink to have fun" (*NJ*, 300). Although she claims she can give it up, her life would be very empty without it.

While the two women, Patricia Morgan and Derry Waters, give Rhoda the possibility and the models for a life that is not confined by the southern stereotypes, it is Charles William Waters whose constant

companionship and affection really help Rhoda survive. He also challenges her notions of the world and opens her eyes to the injustices in
her very closed society. He takes Rhoda to a Klan meeting and cockfight
when she first arrives in Dunleith, Alabama. He gives her books, and he
introduces her to Derry Waters and to the larger world of justice for all
in the South. When he admits to her, despite his plans to marry, that he
is gay, Rhoda does not want to accept that reality. "It was very dangerous, what he told me, and I didn't want to be involved in danger" (*NJ,*
135). Later she comes to understand, "I was not safe enough to grow
into a larger understanding" (*NJ,* 135). Her relationship with Charles
William is a true and abiding friendship. Although her father discour-
ages the relationship, fearing Charles William's unconventional ideas,
Rhoda continues to see him precisely because he does not make the traditional demands upon her. He does not want sex, and he does not want
Rhoda to behave like a southern belle. In fact, he challenges her to be
different, to be more than what most southern men want women to be.
The coda at the end of the novel takes place 30 years later, and Charles
William has just died of a heart condition. Rhoda, thinking back on
their lives, realizes just how much Charles William has really done for
her. Had it not been for him, she would, perhaps, have lost herself
because almost every effort she made to break free was taken over by her
father. "He took dominion everywhere" (*NJ,* 356). Charles William, on
the other hand, offered equality and friendship and art. And it was the
art that saved both Rhoda and Charles William.

A central episode in Rhoda's growth from ignorance to knowledge of
the reality of the South occurs in Alexandria, Louisiana. Rhoda's maid,
Klane Marengo, is accused of killing her cousin over a man, but Klane
and the others present at the card game when Delmonica falls on the
knife say that it is an accident. Klane calls Rhoda, who arranges lawyers
and bail, but just before the trial, Klane's lawyer tells her she must plead
guilty. Apparently, he does not want to be seen pleading for a black
woman. "The mood's not good right now" (*NJ,* 344), the lawyer tells
Rhoda. Rhoda promises help, calls Charles William, and the two call
Derry Waters, who provides a lawyer. However, the outcome is not
happy. Before the lawyer can get to Alexandria, Klane hangs herself,
knowing, as other blacks in the community do, that there is no real possibility of justice for her.

That lesson about the realities of race in the South, perhaps not
learned immediately, is one of the most significant lessons of the novel.
In order to live fully, Rhoda will have to see the deep chasm that exists

between the world in which she has almost total privilege and the other South, the South of her maids. While she is trapped in an unhappy marriage and is constrained by traditions that force women into certain roles, Klane has no freedom at all because the law can take it away at any time. She understands what the lawyer is saying when he tells her she must plead guilty. The gulf between Rhoda's understanding of life and Klane Marengo's is revealed in a conversation between them. Klane tells Rhoda, "Mr. Edmund say I got to plead guilty or they might put me in the electric chair" (*NJ,* 343), but Rhoda's reaction, "I won't let them do it to her. I don't care what she did. She doesn't deserve to be locked up in a jail" (*NJ,* 347), reveals her ignorance and her assumption of privilege. As disempowered as Rhoda is in her relationships with men, she feels deeply empowered where money and influence are concerned; when she arrives at Klane's house to find the woman has hanged herself, she is shocked and cannot understand. Later, she will come to appreciate the deep gulf between the races in the South, but in Alexandria on the day that Klane Marengo dies, she does not.

As Susan Larson notes in the New Orleans *Times Picayune,* Gilchrist has always recognized the dark side of life even as her characters fail to understand what is happening.[3] It is Gilchrist's perspective that saves the novel from pure romanticism. Rhoda wants to love and be loved, and that desire is central to practically everything she does. Even as Klane's body is being cut down, she wants the civil rights lawyer to make love to her, but Gilchrist keeps the focus on the death and plays Rhoda's need off the dark and tragic reality. Rhoda, at age 24, has not broken free. Once again her father comes to get her and flies her home to the family in Dunleith. She still has much to learn and much to suffer before she will be free.

Quest for Self

Both Amanda McCamey and Rhoda Manning have, as young women, overly romanticized notions about themselves. Because *The Annunciation* covers a much longer time period, the book allows for more sweeping changes in Amanda's dreams, goals, and accomplishments. As a woman in her mid-40s, Amanda can certainly make life choices that Rhoda, at the end of *Net of Jewels,* is incapable of making. However, both books, in focusing on the growth of the single character, no matter how embedded that character is in her family and in her social situation, help to focus and define the quest for self. That self for both women is one that can make independent decisions, act on her own needs and desires, and finally, free herself from the crushing weight of family expectations. Rhoda does not achieve that degree of freedom in *Net of Jewels,* but what she has learned during the course of five years has made her aware of ways to achieve it.

Chapter Five
The Family Dynasty

The Anna Papers, I Cannot Get You Close Enough,
and *Starcarbon*

Gilchrist's interest in individual characters has developed over the course of her writing into an interest in individuals' relationships with their families and into an acceptance of a large clan of characters. The southern family, the heart of southern society, becomes in the stories and novels the battleground on which the fight for self is fought. Whereas characters such as Amanda McCamey and Rhoda Manning struggle for independence from families that would force them into the role of the southern belle, characters in other novels approach individual growth through the family. *The Anna Papers* examines the relationships within the Hand clan and illustrates how characters can become themselves while nurturing the bonds of kinship. In *I Cannot Get You Close Enough,* Gilchrist further explores how characters achieve wholeness through the group, and in *Starcarbon,* the balance between individual growth and family connections is made clear.

The Anna Papers

While the theme of overcoming obstacles and finding one's self is one that Gilchrist carries over into her second novel, *The Anna Papers,* published in 1988, this book contains the beginning of the sense of the Hand clan and the recognition of the power of the extended family. Anna Hand, too, has stopped the slippery slide into respectability and gentility in order to become a writer, as Amanda McCamey has done, but Anna's victory is threatened after her death when her sister, the executor of her estate, is horrified by the revelations in Anna's journals and letters. Indeed, Anna's loss of identity is a real threat after death, but Anna's character emerges to change the family focus and to broaden the scope of her influence to several generations of the Hand family.

Gilchrist alternates her novels with her collections of short stories in order to filter the experiences of the longer works through the characters and incidents of the shorter ones, giving both a richness and texture that illuminate them in ways that are almost symbiotic. Readers of the collection *Victory over Japan* have already met Anna Hand and have seen her cool response to Lady Margaret Sarpie. Anna's ability to hold her own against the silly criticism of the New Orleans society matron gives her behavior in *The Anna Papers* an added depth. Further, Anna Hand is seen coming to terms with leaving her lover in "Anna, Part I" in *Drunk with Love*, short stories that were collected after *The Anna Papers*. In "Anna, Part I," the character returns to her writing after a torturous affair with the redheaded, married baby doctor. In the story, Anna goes home, "take[s] herself back from the world" (*DWL,* 222) and begins to write again. Her subject, "start with the tribe" (*DWL,* 222), is her family, the same subject that draws her back to North Carolina in *The Anna Papers;* in fact, the time and the setting are so similar that the short story seems a sketch of the more fully developed novel, even though it was published later. In "Anna, Part I," the redheaded baby doctor, who is so important to Anna in the novel, is given a context, a world, and a wife. In the short story, Anna also accepts her death: "it's all right to die if you've done your work" (*DWL,* 226). Anna, looking back at the books she has written, feels that she has had a voice. In the novel *The Anna Papers,* however, she feels she must write one last book, say one more thing. If the short story is placed beside the novel, a clear connection with *The Anna Papers* emerges, because Anna begins to write a story at the end of "Anna, Part I." She says, "I will create characters and they will tell me my secrets" (*DWL,* 238). She returns to her home, her family, and her writing, and she brings a new member into the tribe.

Another connection between Gilchrist's novel and her collections of short stories is that Anna Hand is Rhoda Manning's cousin, so Anna participates in all of the history of the Manning family that interconnects with the early short stories; that history further deepens the novel's context. In addition, Anna is a lot like her cousin Rhoda. Both are headstrong and independent, both have been married several times, and both have red hair—Anna comments that the redheaded baby doctor looks like her twin brother, so Rhoda's wonderful red hair is repeated in Anna. In fact, although their childhoods are different—Rhoda's family moves during the war while Anna's stays rooted in North Carolina— the older the two women become and the more Gilchrist writes about them, the more their identities merge and intertwine. For both women, writing is the vehicle for self-knowledge, and it frees them from the conventional bonds of love and marriage.

A final connection that links *The Anna Papers* to the rest of Gilchrist's work is the character of the poet Frank Gautier. Several of Gilchrist's stories refer to a dead poet. In *The Age of Miracles,* a poet named Frank Alter has killed himself and his passing indicates the loss of creativity and talent among the poets of New Orleans and among the mourners in Fayetteville. In *The Anna Papers,* Gilchrist seems to be trying to deal with the dead poet through his love for Anna. Had he not died (and there is a hint in the letters found in Anna's house that he may have committed suicide), they would have been married. They would, Anna thinks, have been happy. When Anna thinks of dying, she thinks of seeing Frank again, and death becomes less threatening. Gilchrist, in using the poet as a *leitmotiv* in her books, offers the possibility of immortality, a life that characters throughout Gilchrist's stories and novels are seeking, a way of continuing beyond the frame of the story.

Throughout *The Anna Papers,* Gilchrist returns to Anna's past, the time before Anna became a famous writer and went off to New York, as the present moves ineluctably forward. Of that past, Anna's adolescence in Charlotte, North Carolina, Gilchrist writes, "Anna went to the public high school and was the editor of the yearbook and directed the senior play and was the class poet and the valedictorian and had six different boyfriends every year and could not love them very much."[1] What seems to be coldness in the adolescent becomes the deeply analytical penchant in the writer. Anna tries to see through the veil of tradition and southern family life. The writer then looks back on the childhood of the girl born in 1942, "right in the middle of the Second World War" (*AP,* 22), and she sees the growing family: her sisters Helen and Louise; her brothers James, Niall, and Daniel. She sees "the Old Victorian house on Shannon Street, an old house painted sky blue with white gingerbread and shutters and trim, where the Hand children lived and grew and had their rooms and hid in the attic and the tower" (*AP,* 22). It is Anna's memory of her childhood that brings the Gilchrist clans together—the Mannings, the McGruders, the Hands. These memories sustain the actions in the novel's three sections.

As the oldest Hand child, Anna was the leader during childhood, the protector of her younger brothers and sisters, but in 1984 she sees those same brothers and sisters "chained to their jobs and their husbands and wives and ex-wives and children and habits and ideas and fears, closed and open doors and spidery corners. Who will save the Hand children now and set them free?" (*AP,* 24). So Anna, famous writer, exile in New York, decides to return to Charlotte to free her family, and the freedom she brings is more vast than she or any of them ever expected.

The novel falls into three segments: Anna's quest for her niece Olivia, her family's grief over Anna's suicide, and her sister Helen's response to being Anna's literary executor. Even after her death, the effect of Anna's influence on her family is enormous.

Part I, entitled "Anna," focuses the novel on Anna's quest for her niece Olivia—her brother Daniel's daughter—and her quest for love. She is in love with a redheaded baby doctor in New York who is married and will not leave his wife, so Anna leaves the city and goes home to Charlotte, taking with her a letter from a young girl named Olivia de Havilland Hand, her 16-year-old half-Cherokee niece who lives with her Indian relatives in Tahlequah, Oklahoma.

In the summer of 1967, Daniel Hand met Summer Waggoner in California and married her. He brought her back to North Carolina to meet his family, but the young woman felt ostracized by the insular Hand clan and left Daniel to go back to Oklahoma where she died giving birth to Daniel's child. Neither Daniel nor Summer knew when she left that she was carrying their child. The only thing the child Olivia has of the Hand family is the name, which links her to Anna Hand, whose work the girl discovers in an English class. Olivia writes to Anna, and a relationship blossoms. Olivia must be put into the family history, Anna decides, and, despite Daniel's misgivings, she goes to Oklahoma to visit the girl. This journey resembles Guy's trip in *The Annunciation* to find the daughter Amanda had given up for adoption. The lost children in Gilchrist's fiction must be returned to their families.

In Olivia and in her half-sister Jessie, Daniel's other 16-year-old daughter, Anna Hand sees the possibility of freedom that her generation of women did not often achieve. Olivia, as she tells Daniel, is "amazing, self-protective" (*AP,* 97). She is a girl who can take care of herself, but Anna is still worried—despite her efforts to free herself from traditional notions of how women should live and be treated—and exhorts her brother to bring his daughter to North Carolina. "She belongs to us. We can't leave her there [in Oklahoma]. There isn't a man to protect her. Her grandfather is old. There should be a man" (*AP,* 97). In fact, despite Anna's protestations of freedom, she reverts to the southern view of protecting the women. It is a family view of men and women that makes women dependent upon men, even as Anna herself struggles to be independent. Anna finally convinces Daniel to meet his daughter and sets the wheels for family acceptance in motion. Before her death, she brings the tribe together.

Shortly after Olivia comes to North Carolina, 43-year-old Anna discovers she has breast cancer. She responds to that diagnosis by saying, "I have lived my life. I have not forgotten to be alive. I was glad to be here" (*AP,* 144), and that response signals her intention just as clearly as does her philosophy that "matter is neither created nor destroyed. All I'm going to do is shut down a system" (*AP,* 143). Her suicide, once again mirroring the suicide of the poet, is a way of controlling destiny, of deciding how to die. Anna's own grandfather, on finding he had cancer, had hung himself, and Anna too decides when and how to die. Anna had seldom been able to control how she lived. Until it was too late, she could not get the redheaded, married, baby doctor to leave his wife and marry her; she could not change her family; and she could not control her body, whose cancerous growths betrayed her. Her death, though, as her sister Helen understands, was Anna's choice. "She had a right to her death" (*AP,* 154), Helen tells her grieving brothers, who are busy saying they will never forgive Anna for leaving them the way she did.

With Anna's death, the other women in the family must take on new roles. Helen, Anna's executor, is the one who changes most. It is almost as if Anna, wanting her conventional younger sister to free herself of the constricting society of the Junior League and the family, wills her several boxes of stories and papers to force Helen to view the world in an entirely different manner. The mantle of freedom is passed on from older sister to younger.

The papers themselves become Helen's responsibility. She asks herself, "Why did she make me executor? I don't want this job" (*AP,* 207). She fears her own mother's embarrassment at what she has found, and she is horrified that Anna has used what their mother calls Helen's voice. Helen feels violated by her sister's appropriation and feels her identity slipping away under her dead sister's power. She even complains, "I have never been this chatty and never gossipped [*sic*] in my life" (*AP,* 208). How, then, can Helen reclaim herself and move beyond the image she fears in her sister's writing? Gilchrist's own style in this novel is chatty and gossipy, so the fact that Helen, who is also chatty and gossipy, becomes more of a voice does lend her authority and definition because, at times, she seems to speak for the author.

The more she reads, the more Helen begins to understand the sister who was always a part of her life; in fact, it is Anna who finally gives

Helen her freedom. As she reads through her sister's papers, the embarrassment passes, and Helen begins to visualize Anna's notion of freedom clearly defined. Of Anna's sense of freedom, Helen notes, "She thought about it all the time, talked about it, brooded upon ways it could be taken from her. She knew too much about our family to ever let down her guard a moment" (*AP,* 221).

Conventionality wars with independence in Helen. Many times she thinks she will simply destroy the papers Anna has left because they say so many negative things about the family. Her mother, also a very conventional woman, urges her to "throw [Anna's work] away" (*AP,* 247). In the end, however, Helen preserves the papers and, in doing so, gives herself an opportunity to grow away from the confining role of wife, mother, and dutiful daughter. She meets the other executor, John Carmichel, the poet whom everyone calls Mike, and admits to him that reading Anna's papers has changed her. "I don't think I'm the same person I was a month ago" (*AP,* 254), she tells Mike, and the meaning of that is pregnant with possibilities.

A woman who has never been unfaithful to her husband, Helen nevertheless sleeps with her coexecutor almost immediately and begins to free herself from her own past notions of fidelity and femininity. Even her old boyfriend and distant cousin, Phelan Manning, notices the change and wants her to run away with him to Africa. Helen has finally extricated herself from her old notions of responsibility, and she can promise herself that she will go to Boston and spend time with her poet.

The Anna Papers contains moments of real wit, as when Helen's daughter DeDe calls to say she is pregnant and wants to come home to Charlotte. Helen, just having freed herself from all her demanding children, tells her husband Spencer that he has to take care of the problem. Lying in bed with her lover, Helen receives her husband's call and tells him, "I'm busy, Spencer. We don't have much time to do this" (*AP,* 261). He thinks she is referring to working on Anna's papers, but Helen could just as easily mean she doesn't have much time for her affair because the poet Mike has to go back to Boston. Spencer, who has never heard his wife talk this way, is confused by the change in her behavior, but the sexual innuendo allows the reader to be privy to her newfound freedom.

The large southern family also comes in for playful criticism. Of her five children and all her nieces and nephews, Helen thinks, "some days I wish I'd strangled them in their cribs" (*AP,* 235), a comment that certainly undercuts all her expressed notions of the importance of children and family.

As *The Anna Papers* develops, it becomes clear that the focus on women—their inner lives, their beliefs and convictions, their conflicts and jealousies—is at the heart of Gilchrist's anatomy of the Hand family. Anna herself is laid bare without the structuring censorship of authorial comment. She is bodily on each page until her death, and she lingers after in her papers and in the ghost that, several times, reveals herself to Helen.

I Cannot Get You Close Enough

Related to *The Anna Papers* in terms of characters and themes is *I Cannot Get You Close Enough,* published in 1990. It is a collection of three novellas about the Hand family and their friends. The Carl Jung epigraph, "Generally speaking, all the life which the parents could have lived, but of which they thwarted themselves for artificial motives, is passed on to the children in substitute form,"[2] sets the tone for the three pieces in the book. All are about the children of Anna's siblings, and all illustrate how those children deal with family history and parental legacies. Gilchrist adds an ironic epigraph to the serious Carl Jung one, a couplet from Philip Larkin: "They fuck you up, your mum and dad. / They may not mean to but they do" (*CE,* vi). This humorous comment suggests the Hand tragicomedy and mitigates the heavy-handed message of the Jung quotation; however, it is clear from both epigraphs that Gilchrist intends to study the effects that parents have on their children and the ways in which children fight to free themselves from family entanglements.

The novellas are in a sense the legacy of Anna Hand, the "repository of family secrets and disreputable stories"[3] for the Hand family. At the end of *The Anna Papers,* many members of the Hand family are concerned about what Anna's papers might contain and what might be revealed that they would rather keep secret. That book raises the issue of what in the papers is fiction and what is family history. Looking over the papers, Helen comes across a story of Phelan Manning and Anna and cannot tell whether the affair Anna writes about actually happened or whether Anna made it up and "used their names because she was too lazy to make up fiction ones" (*AP,* 211). Helen's concern about what might be true and what might not and about how the papers should be read is one that both the reader and the writer of fiction are constantly confronting. As McDonnell says, "*The Anna Papers* thus raises many issues concerning writing, fiction-making, fictionalizing, memory, storytelling, and gossip" (McDonnell, 187), and the stories in *I Cannot Get You Close Enough* deal with the same issues. Anna Hand's pen is in much of that book, and her sense of the story, the history of the family, the tragedy that she feels is a part of the Hand legacy, are all played out in the lives of her nieces, cousins, and distant relatives. The Hands and the Mannings meet in the novellas in a more structured familial way than they have in any other book, and their interrelationships and interdependencies are chronicled and dissected. The inner workings of both families are thus uncovered, and family myth is painstakingly separated from the realities that the younger generation must face.

The first novella, "Winter," is frankly in the voice of Anna. It is "a manuscript that the deceased poet and novelist Anna Hand left in a suitcase in a rented cottage in Beddiford, Maine [almost certainly a reference to the actual town of Biddeford]" (*CE,* 3), just before she kissed her redheaded baby doctor lover and went off to kill herself. It is the story of Anna's quest to save her brother Daniel's daughter Jessie from her mother, Sheila, whom Anna considers "mean, destructive, spoiled, dangerous, unprincipled, remorseless" (*CE,* 3).

Sheila MacNiece, the only daughter of a family that loved money but nothing and nobody else, is a sort of female Snopes posing as a southern belle. Anna observes that there was not one time "in her life when she wasn't perfectly turned out, dressed and manicured and coiffed" (*CE,* 8). The irony is that Sheila is a southern belle on drugs, and her interest in the traditions of her family and her community is undercut by her grasping acquisitive nature. She cannot mother and she cannot love. She can only use her child to get money from her ex-husband. As it turns out, Anna discovers that Sheila has had and deserted another child, confirming the Hand suspicions that Sheila is incapable of love.

Sheila's daughter Jessie is, on the other hand, a wonderful, bright, shining child, "my heart, my dearest, most precious little child," (*CE,* 5). Thus, early in the story, two dichotomies are established. Like Rhoda Manning, Jessie must fight against her mother to survive, and Anna Hand plans to help her in that effort. Further, the difference between the mother and the daughter is, in a sense, Anna's perception of the difference between the Hands and the MacNieces. The battle between those who are blessed with Hand DNA, as Anna is constantly referring to it, and those who lack Hand qualities is, once again, the object of Anna Hand's preoccupation. It is, she believes, "Jessie's own power and light, which she had inherited from Daniel" (*CE,* 84), that makes Jessie one of them, a Hand. She is not a MacNiece, one of the clan who have always perceived enemies all around them (*CE*, 84). Jessie is, like Anna, a free spirit, a young woman who will survive and who will free herself of the taint of the MacNieces.

The central conflict of the novella, however, a conflict that relates it to much of Gilchrist's other fiction, is the conflict between Sheila's view of life and Anna's. The two women are, in this piece, representative of two views of women in the South. Sheila is the Old South; she is all the women who are "weak and defenseless, and have men in [their] power" (*CE*, 22). She is the destructive female force, the woman who uses men and destroys them. Anna is, on the other hand, the independent woman, the artist, the free spirit who may drive men away but who never stops loving them. She finds her own way and identifies herself without reference to the confining definitions of the Old South.

The history of Sheila's relationship with Daniel Hand is explained in one paragraph in "Winter," and this clarification allows Gilchrist to juxtapose free women with dependent women. The explanation also clarifies and makes the ages of Olivia de Havilland Hand and Jessie Hand understandable. This clarification is central not only to the next novella in *I Cannot Get You Close Enough* but also to *The Anna Papers,* and helps define the relationships among all the Hand offspring. In light of the Hand family history, it is understandable why Anna must rescue Jessie from her mother.

Sheila, as a debutante, leads Daniel on as her beau, but drops him at her debutante ball for Darley Mahew, a fortune-hunter in search of a rich southern girl, and goes away to Switzerland with Darley for the summer. Daniel, in despair, goes out West to be a hippie, meets and marries Summer Deer Waggoner, and brings her home to Charlotte to meet his family. Summer finds the Hands overwhelming and runs back home to her reservation in Oklahoma. She is pregnant, but none of the Hands know about that then, nor do they for the next 15 years.

Meanwhile, Sheila returns home to Charlotte, and Daniel, in despair over Summer's departure, goes to Sheila for comfort and gets her pregnant. Both fathers arrange to annul Daniel's marriage to Summer and marry him to Sheila. Seven months later, Jessie is born, but three months before Jessie's birth Olivia is born and her mother dies. Although the two births are not essential to "Winter," Gilchrist inserts the story here to prepare for the next novella and to gloss *The Anna Papers* in a way that clarifies the motivation for Anna's preoccupation with Olivia.

"Winter" explains how Daniel, in love with Summer, marries Sheila. Soon dissatisfied with Daniel, with motherhood, and with her life, Sheila leaves her husband and her daughter to marry a Rothchild. That marriage also disintegrates, and Sheila, after two-and-one-half years, decides she wants Jessie back. That scenario focuses the action of the novella and justifies Anna's determination to keep Sheila away from her niece.

Anna's analysis of Sheila is trenchant and very damning. Describing Sheila's bid for her daughter, Anna says, "she goes home to Charlotte, makes up with her folks, sets up housekeeping, starts going to church, does some good works with Big Ed's [her father's] money" (CE, 60), and then expects to have Jessie as a reward. Anna further observes of Sheila, "you can see what she is up to and you still can't stop her" (CE, 60). That attitude is how all the Hands, and especially Anna, felt about Sheila when she was an adolescent. They saw her snaring Daniel, but they could not stop her.

Like the black widow spider, the deadly southern belle destroys all who come in contact with her. Sheila will surely destroy Jessie if she wins the custody battle, so Anna must find a way to stop her. Her efforts take her to Turkey, where Sheila has had a child by a Turkish communist and abandoned the baby boy. This is the information that will save Jessie. This information proves that Sheila is an unfit mother.

Looking back over the episode, Anna muses, "I believe life is supposed to be tragic, why else would we need whiskey or need God?" (CE, 86). However, the episode that comes so close to being tragic is saved by Anna precisely because she has the strength and independence to fight for her niece. Even her brother Daniel worries that she should not go to Turkey alone, but her trip uncovers the vital information needed to save the Hand clan.

As in *The Anna Papers*, Anna is the savior, the one who holds the family together. It is not the Hand brothers and father, but the sisters and the mother who are strong. Of her own mother and father, Anna observes, "she is tougher than he is. . . . If I told her we were going to have Sheila killed she would take it better than Daddy would" (CE, 79). Anna, too, is stronger than Daniel, and her urge to protect him and his daughter is what drives her.

Chronologically, Anna does not yet know about the child Olivia, but when she learns about the girl, she will be just as fierce in Olivia's defense and protection. Anna's protection blankets all the clan. She observes about her family and herself, "things which are bearable in my life are unbearable to me in the lives of my family. I cannot bear to watch them suffer" (CE, 86). That feeling is what motivates her to help her brother Daniel keep his child.

The second novella fleshes out much of what Gilchrist writes in *The Anna Papers* about Olivia de Havilland Hand. Ironically, an interview in *Publishers Weekly* reveals that, as Gilchrist got more "involved with this extended Hand-Manning family, she found that short fiction was no longer a comfortable genre" (Smith, 46). Yet she uses a form halfway between the short story and the novel to create background and lives for characters who grow in importance in her fictional world. In *I Cannot Get You Close Enough,* she uses that hybrid form to create stories from another point of view, and the novella, "De Havilland Hand," is a vehicle for giving Olivia a past, a history for the family album, and a voice of her own.

Olivia learns that, in the mid-sixties, the young Daniel Hand and the young Summer Deer Waggoner spent an idyllic summer in San Francisco, and then Daniel's money ran out and the young couple, just married, flew to Charlotte to meet the Hands. She understands Summer's anxiety that the clan might not like her because she, too, has suffered from that same anxiety. Olivia's experience helps her to sympathize with her mother who, in just ten days, was on her way home to Oklahoma, "with sixty dollars in her pocket and enough rage to keep her heart from breaking" (*CE,* 98). Later Summer admits to a friend in Memphis, "I wish I'd killed his mother and maybe Helen" (*CE,* 99), so it appears that the clan has closed ranks against Olivia's mother. In *The Anna Papers,* Daniel implies in a conversation with Anna that Summer felt shunned, but her motivation is never entirely clear in the novel. To the two conventional Hand women—Mrs. Hand and Helen, already Helen Abadie, married to a banker and having children of her own—the exotic Summer Deer must seem an inappropriate match for Daniel Hand, but Olivia, looking at her mother's experience from a distance of 16 years, can see her loneliness.

On the way home to Oklahoma, Summer Deer finds out she is pregnant. Because all her friends tell her she can get money from the government for the baby, she decides to keep it but she dies in childbirth. The baby, named Olivia de Havilland because of a movie Summer saw on her way back to the reservation, is given to Mary Lily, Summer's younger sister, to rear. Mary Lily is too fat to get a man, so Olivia's grandfather, Little Sun, gives the child to her.

Through a sequence of events, Gilchrist brings Olivia closer and closer to knowledge of her father, until the girl finally discovers her aunt Anna Hand and writes to her. Gilchrist carefully structures the child's growing awareness of her family outside the Oklahoma reservation.

Books open the world to Olivia, and when she finds she has an aunt who is a famous writer, she pursues her with letters as she dreams of the father she has never seen.

As in some of her short stories, Gilchrist develops the same scene from two perspectives. In *The Anna Papers,* she shows the meeting between Anna and Olivia from Anna's point of view; in "De Havilland Hand," she views the scene from the perspective of the 16-year-old niece. Like a film that is speeded up, their first weekend together rolls by, followed by more waiting, a trip to North Carolina, and then Anna's suicide. Because these events had already been described in *The Anna Papers,* the scenes in "De Havilland Hand" are reviewed from Olivia's point of view so the reader can see the impact of events on the young woman.

The second novella also brings Olivia to school in North Carolina, the land on which her Cherokee ancestors lived before the Trail of Tears. In an unmailed letter to her father, Olivia, in her anger at him, speaks of North Carolina: "I guess you know the whole state of North Carolina belonged to the Cherokee nation until they were sent out on the Trail of Tears" (*CE,* 124). He has his wealth, his land, and his family, and he has kept it all from her, just as his ancestors had cheated hers a century earlier.

Despite her anger at the perceived injustice, Olivia feels bereft of family and so tries to find a way to make the stranger-father love her. Her solution is to pretend she is an A student, and that does work for a time. Olivia moves to North Carolina to go to school, carrying with her a forged transcript. When the forgery is discovered and Olivia can no longer keep up the facade, the Hands, recognizing her vulnerability, rally around her and bring her into the heart of the family. With that acceptance, she loses, at least for a time, her connection with her past, and thinking back on her life in Oklahoma, she muses, "I guess that's my childhood I have to leave behind" (*CE,* 197).

A rite of passage story, "De Havilland Hand" contains elements of what makes Gilchrist's stories about children so poignant. All her young people teeter between innocence and awareness. They hang delicately on the cusp of adulthood, making forays into the land of sexual activity and then retreating back into the innocence that glimmers around Gilchrist's young women. Olivia is at the same time adult and child. Her reservation boyfriend Bobby Tree comments that she seems 20 or 25, but standing in her gym shorts in the principal's office in North Carolina with a forged transcript on the desk in front of her, she is a vulnerable child.

The final novella in *I Cannot Get You Close Enough* is also about young people of the Hand-Manning clan. "A Summer in Maine" places Olivia and Jessie together with Crystal Manning Weiss's children King Mallison and Crystal Anne Weiss and Andria (the maid Traceleen's niece) in Maine where all confront what it means to enter adulthood. Told from many perspectives, the novella moves among the voices of the adults and the young people. Traceleen focuses on the theme of all the novellas and especially of "A Summer in Maine" when she observes, "They grow up fast, the young ones that we love. Before long all we have are memories and they are gone out to the world" (*CE*, 214). Indeed, Gilchrist, in *I Cannot Get You Close Enough,* is not writing simply about children, but about the delicate balance between the lives of children and the lives of the adults who care for them. All three novellas help illuminate for Gilchrist and for her readers the intricate interconnections of family, friends, and loved ones. It is in this book that Gilchrist is most conscious of connections between the stories of several different clans. In "A Summer in Maine," all the clans leave their special territories—New Orleans, North Carolina, Arkansas, Seattle—to meet on unfamiliar ground and make new and different connections. Crystal, at a strained point in her marriage to Manny Weiss; Lydia, friend of Crystal and an artist between lovers and between creative projects; Traceleen, competent and caring nurturer to all: these are the adults who watch the next generation glisten in the Maine summer and see all the adolescents grow into new beings before their eyes. The young people also have voices in the text. Jessie, King, Olivia, Andria, and Crystal Anne discover ways of speaking about experience that help them understand the nature of their living in the families they find themselves in.

This capacity to speak is important because all have, to one extent or another, suffered from abuse by the adults in their lives. Jessie's mother deserted her; King, estranged from his father, assigns himself the role of Manny Weiss's stepson; Olivia has had to negotiate between two families and two very different worlds; Andria has suffered the abuse and neglect of an alcoholic mother; and Crystal Anne has watched her parents fight, her mother have affairs, and her half-brother escape into drugs and liquor. None has had the quiet, idyllic childhood that Gilchrist speaks of in *Falling through Space,* but all struggle with the childhood given them and manage to make some meaning out of it.

Although all the characters have a voice, and even Anna Hand's voice comes back from the dead with a poetic message about love and loss, it is Traceleen whose voice holds the novella together. She also holds the summer together as various people come and go, causing disruption and leaving unhappiness in their wake.

As Traceleen points out, "The main love affair of the end of June was between King and Jessie" (*CE, 306*). Even though Jessie's father, Daniel Hand, extracted from King a sort of southern chivalric vow not to sleep with Jessie, King cannot keep that promise, and that failure precipitates a series of actions that have their consequences in the lives of many characters and in later novels.

But despite Traceleen's seeing it as the main love affair, the Jessie-King union is not the only one. In fact, the novella is focused on how people love because that is the way they get "close enough," but Anna Hand's message hints that love does not always have that effect: "I cannot get you close enough, I said to him, pitiful as a child, and never can and never will. We cannot get from anyone else the things we need to fill the endless terrible need, not to be dissolved, not to sink back into sand, heat, broom, air, thinnest air. And so we revolve around each other and our dreams collide" (*CE, 387*). The way Jessie and King try to get "close enough" results in her pregnancy, marriage, and finally, unhappiness.

Others choose more independent options. Andria says, "No man is going to take over my life and start getting me in the kitchen cooking and washing dishes" (*CE, 384*). She, like Olivia, wants her freedom, and sees love and marriage as confining. She wants to finish high school, go to Baton Rouge to the university, and live her own life. Olivia's solution is to save money; she tells Jessie to save money and never to have any more children. The vast difference between the two independent young women's expectations for their futures and King's is chilling. King says, "I love Jessie. I told her I did. I just can't stand to stay here" (*CE, 391*). He feels hemmed in and confined by the consequences of his love, but Andria and Olivia feel vitally alive and interested in the future as a consequence of the choices they have made.

And Traceleen closes the book with "This too shall pass away" (*CE, 391*). Her understanding and acceptance allow all the characters the freedom to make mistakes and the maturity to accept the consequences of their choices. Those choices are especially important for women, because the choices are the means by which they free and define themselves. That Andria and Olivia choose action rather than passive acceptance of the situation, as Jessie does, illustrates the dichotomy between the women who, like Rhoda and Anna, grasp at possibilities and the women who accept the traditional role of wife and mother. Jessie is, indeed, the most unhappy character at the end of the book. Because her unhappiness has the effect of driving King even further away from her, she is doubly unhappy.

I Cannot Get You Close Enough looks both backward to novels and short stories Gilchrist has already published and forward to other novels and stories. It is the perfect linking text, written when Gilchrist was looking more and more toward the novel form but also searching for a way to integrate characters and information about her growing fictional clans into a larger structure. In this group of three novellas, Gilchrist brings people together to see just how close they can get and then shows that, no matter how close the family, no matter how passionate the love, no one can really get close enough.

Starcarbon

Several times in stories and novels, Gilchrist has referred to particularly scintillating young women by comparing them to starcarbon, the element that constitutes the stars, the building blocks of the universe. Olivia de Havilland Hand is referred to in that manner in *I Cannot Get You Close Enough,* and the idea, so dear to Anna Hand, that we are all of the same substance and slip back into the sand and the sea and the stars, strengthens the notion that all parts of the universe are related and that people have intimate connections with each other. All people contain the components of starcarbon. These celestial connections are central to Gilchrist's fiction and especially to the novel *Starcarbon,* published in 1994, because Olivia must come to terms with the two sides of her family and reconcile the conflicting notions of self that each side has set out for her. She must integrate, rather than separate, the two components of her family background.

As in her other books, the characters in *Starcarbon* walk in and out of other novels and stories, confirming the interconnectedness of all Gilchrist's fictional lives. Jessie, Daniel Hand's other 19-year-old daughter, is now married to Crystal Manning Weiss's son King Mallison, and she has just had a son. Little Sun, Olivia's Cherokee grandfather who appeared in *The Anna Papers,* has an important role and message in *Starcarbon.* Bobby Gilbert Tree, Olivia's early love who returns from Montana to try to win Olivia back from her Anglo relatives, becomes more important as the novel develops. As Gilchrist has commented in many interviews, her characters often insist on a voice and push their way into stories and novels. Some who start out as minor characters become more

significant with each new work, and that is certainly true of Bobby Tree
and Little Sun.

In this novel, as in *Net of Jewels,* Gilchrist links personal events with
large and cataclysmic social issues. The civil rights movement is an
appropriate emblem for the quest for freedom that Rhoda undertakes in
Net of Jewels. Similarly, in *Starcarbon,* the events of Olivia's summer in
Tahlequah, Oklahoma, where she returns to further explore her Cherokee family, are mirrored in the crumbling of the Soviet Union and in the
cataclysms of nature that threaten to overwhelm people. Tornadoes
sweep across the landscape, families break down, people assert their
independence, and new alliances and connections must be forged. As
the novel opens, it is 1991, and "a long strange summer is about to
begin. For the world, for political history, and for one particular member
of our species. One sweet, funny, driven, brown-eyed nineteen-year-old
Scorpio named Olivia de Havilland Hand."[4]

While accepting interconnection, the characters in *Starcarbon* also
insist on their individual identity and their place in the world, their separateness, and it is this insistence that focuses the novel. All seem to
agree that "Everything is connected to everything else," but they also
complain, "God, I am so sick of being lonely and alone" (*S,* 65); that
refrain echoes not only throughout this novel, but throughout most of
Gilchrist's fiction. The goal in *Starcarbon* is to find a way to be alone
without being lonely or to be with people and not feel alone, and Olivia
finds the perfect balance in imagination. Daniel Hand notes of her that
"she had imagination, the most seductive of all gifts. . . . It was this gift
that reminded the Hand family of their lost Anna. In her generation it
had been Anna who dreamed up and proposed the games the Hand
children played. In this generation it was Olivia" (*S,* 163). Olivia revital-
izes "the stodgier children in the family" and brings the "fabulous and
exotic" into their lives. (*S,* 163).

But Olivia cannot simply dispense imagination; she herself needs love,
affection, and guidance. Unfortunately, the Hands are too depleted to
give it to her. "Anna was dead and Helen had run off and left her family
for a poet" (*S,* 45). Daniel Hand is drinking too much, and none of the
others is capable of giving Olivia any sense of direction. In *Starcarbon,* the
traditional southern family is showing its frayed edges, and Olivia must
return to her Indian roots to find real meaning in her life, to learn, as her
psychiatrist tells her, "to be alone and not be lonely" (*S,* 136).

Starcarbon treats many of the themes central to Gilchrist's fiction in a
more dense and complex way. In this novel, the solutions that Rhoda

Manning, Amanda McCamey, and Anna Hand sought in order to free themselves from the bonds of family and from the strictures of southern society do not apply to Olivia. She must find a way to live with the family she has found. She, at 19, has achieved the freedom that it takes other Gilchrist women three or four decades to achieve, but she needs to find a way to love and find connections to ground her natural independence.

Olivia admits, "I don't know what love is" (*S,* 263), and she struggles to understand and to separate her feelings from her passionate sexual relationship with Bobby Tree. Her quest to understand her moods and her connections with others is aided by Georgia Jones, a woman who, like Patricia Morgan and Derry Waters in *Net of Jewels,* has a sense of herself. Even though she has given up her profession as a physician and is struggling with a difficult affair and with the horrid children of her lover, Georgia, Olivia's summer school teacher, does provide a sympathetic ear and acts as a surrogate mother to Olivia in her loneliness. It is Georgia who reveals the paradox of her own and of Olivia's lives. Both love and want relationships, but both need to be alone; they need to make their own decisions. Finally, Georgia recommends to Olivia, "tell the truth as fast as you can" (*S,* 296), and that seems to be a way for both women to reconcile the conflicts in their lives.

The terrible paradox of relationships is that the characters seek them out for love, but often end up trapped and stifled in them. When people, even with the best intentions and with love, try to help the ones they care for, they often hurt them. For Gilchrist, the conflict that surrounds the greatest quest, the quest for connection, is often irresolvable. Georgia loves Zach, but his twin sons, hating her for displacing their mother, actually try to kill her. King Mallison loves Jessie, but feeling trapped and inadequate, he dreams of dying. Olivia loves Bobby, but she needs to go on a lightning walk to be alone before she can decide if she will go with him to Montana instead of back to school in North Carolina. Little Sun loves his children but hides from them the money he has just acquired from his oil rights because he fears that the money will ruin them. Money has certainly ruined many of the Hands; it kept Rhoda Manning tied to her father for much too long, and it makes people careless and unhappy. Little Sun says, "it [money] will kill our strength and sap us" (*S,* 206). Olivia relays that comment to Jessie, and she, having had money all her life, opines, "Maybe he's right" (*S,* 206).

Before the events of the summer of 1991 can come together and before all the characters can finally accept each other, each must clear

the ground: "August 19, 1991. On the plain west of Tahlequah a tornado was forming. To be more exact, several tornados, gathering their
winds, their stones, their sand, their insects and leaves and water, getting ready to head down Tornado Alley and clear some ground" (*S,* 277).
While the tornado is forming, the Soviet Union is falling apart and Gor-
bachev is removed from power. Nature, the world, and Gilchrist's characters must reform, reshape alliances and loves, and must begin again.

What gives *Starcarbon* its richness and complexity is the intricate
blending of the romantic with the real. Many of Gilchrist's characters,
most notably Nora Jane Whittington, Alisha Terrebone, and the young
Rhoda Manning, are incurable romantics. The characters in *Starcarbon,*
through hard soul-searching, come to balance their romantic notions
with the real world. In *Starcarbon,* "coming to terms with chaos, accepting the messy business of living and loving and then going on,"[5] is the
central philosophical quest. The tornado cuts a swath through Tahlequah, and everyone is changed by it. They stand awed by the destruction, but from that chaos come love and community.

After the tornado, Bess, the quarter horse Olivia has ridden since
childhood, is found in a cistern just holding her head above the water.
Everyone works together to free her, and that struggle unites all the
parts of Olivia's heritage. Her father, who has come to Tahlequah for a
visit, Bobby Tree, Little Sun, and Olivia all pull together to rescue the
horse, an effort that makes them equals, makes them partners. Olivia is
made whole, her two halves connected by the work in consort to repair
the damage nature has wrought.

Gilchrist structures *Starcarbon* to end at the beginning, to continue
the circle of life. Helen Hand is pregnant by the poet she met in *The
Anna Papers,* so her life, in effect, begins again. At the beginning of *Starcarbon,* old James Hand, the patriarch of the clan, watching his granddaughter, Katherine Elizabeth Hand, play soccer, marvels, "what a
miraculous child" (*S,* 10); at the end, Helen's poet husband begins his
novel with that same "miraculous child," repeating again, in fiction, the
same gestures, "the quick intake of breath, the muscles tightening, then
letting go" (*S,* 305). Life goes on, the old are recreated in the young, and
dreams still occur, even in a world of chaos and uncertainty. Love makes
life possible, and truth.

Expanding Horizons

The progression of Gilchrist's long fiction is seen in the complexity of
each of her novels. *The Annunciation* is the most traditional in structure

and style, and the character of Amanda McCamey is quite like Alisha Terrebone and other Gilchrist romantics, who create their lives out of an image they have of how life is lived in the movies or in novels. *The Anna Papers* challenges some of the southern notions that Amanda McCamey fought so hard to overcome, and the darkness at the center of the novel is larger and more insistent. Anna's death casts a shadow over the book from the beginning, so the notions of freedom and escape are all tinged with the knowledge that any options are temporary and that life itself is finite. *I Cannot Get You Close Enough* challenges both the short story and the novel forms to reconfigure fictional space in a way that allows the past to flow into the present and allows characters to move freely in and out of the past. That reconfiguration also challenges traditional notions of society and culture, so the characters are freer to make their own lives. With *Net of Jewels* and *Starcarbon,* Gilchrist consciously focuses fictional events in a nonfictional context. Rhoda's romantic struggle is carried on within the context of a very real struggle of a people for their freedom. The external reality of the civil rights movement helps Rhoda grow beyond her immature self-absorption, and it critiques the values that made her that way. In *Starcarbon,* Olivia, always a bit outside the confining locus of the southern family, must find a place for herself. Her search for order is mirrored in the world events around her. Gilchrist chooses the collapse of the Soviet Union to resonate with the collapse of the Hand family and with the possibilities for future freedom that are both hoped for and very uncertain.

All Gilchrist's novels grow in both structure and form, and certain themes display consistency as well as development. As in the short stories, the women are the centers of the novels. Their quest for romance, love, freedom, and a sense of self is depicted sympathetically but often with irony. The need for a strong, nurturing mother who herself has asserted her personhood becomes more and more insistent as Gilchrist's novelistic world expands and becomes more complex. Olivia at 19 has already challenged and overcome many of the obstacles that held Amanda McCamey back, and which, ironically, threaten to keep Jessie Manning Mallison from asserting her independence.

As the circle of the family widens to include community, nation, and world, Gilchrist's characters also broaden their horizons and move into new relationships and new communities of love and responsibility. The exclusionary quests of Amanda McCamey and Rhoda Manning in *The Annunciation* and *Net of Jewels* become inclusionary journeys in *The Anna Papers, I Cannot Get You Close Enough,* and *Starcarbon.* Helen learns of her sister's deep and abiding love of the family even as she sought escape in her fiction. It is Anna's sense of family that finally frees Helen from the stultifying burden and responsibility she has imposed on herself with regard to her husband and children. She does not run from her family so much as she finds a new way to accept its members. All the Hands are learning to find ways to fit with each other, and in *Starcarbon,* Olivia succeeds in linking the two halves of her past. She reconciles who she is and what she wants to be with both the Indian and the southern notions of family and community, and in that reconciliation she can become truly herself.

Interview with Ellen Gilchrist

This interview was the result of a series of questions Mary McCay asked Ellen Gilchrist, by mail in early 1996. Gilchrist wrote out her answers to the questions. A telephone conversation broadened the range of the interview slightly and cleared up some questions. Gilchrist preferred a written interview in which she could develop her ideas in a more formal way.

MM: You seem to be creating a female Yoknapatawpha County with your matrilineal families (the McCameys, the Hands, and the Mannings). How do you see those women changing southern culture?

EG: I don't see them as anything but characters in the constant flux of life in "its immensity and wonder."

MM: Your childhood, as depicted in the journals *Falling through Space*, seems to have been very happy, yet the children of your fiction are often very unhappy. Where does the impulse to write about unhappy children come from? Where do you get your stories?

EG: I am extremely empathic and have a huge imagination. I re-create reality imaginatively. Whenever I write about characters, I enter their lives imaginatively, and characters I create are recreations of highly emotional states that I turn into characters. I am just as much Freddy Harwood as I am Anna Hand.

MM: What writers were the center of your childhood reading? What of their view of the world has stuck with you?

EG: I read books day and night. No one author influenced me. I loved good books of all kinds and especially poetry. I adored Edna St. Vincent Millay and memorized most of her poetry from reading it so often. Also, Emily Dickinson and T. S. Eliot and huge reams of British poetry. God knows what all that poetry did to me, but it certainly made music in my head.

MM: Could you discuss your participation in your Shakespeare reading group.

EG: I have a group of friends who come to my house once a week and we read the plays out loud. If there are more than five or six of us, we don't get to read enough, so we keep it very private and silly, and we love doing it and have read many plays many, many times. We thought it up one boring summer night about eight years ago. That night we read *King Lear*. It took four and a half hours.

MM: You said once that you never tried to write when you had children. How did it feel not to be a writer, to have all your creative energy directed at your sons?

EG: When I had children, I was passionately involved in their lives and my friends, and I had an exciting, eventful life. I read all the time. It gives me the same pleasure as writing. Reading and writing are the same activity if the book is good enough—the one you're writing or reading.

MM: Could you discuss your relationship with Lost Roads Press, Frank Stanford, Ginny Stanford, and C. D. Wright? Could you also discuss your support of the *Barataria Review* in the mid-seventies?

EG: Frank was a close friend of mine and introduced me to Ginny, whom I love and admire. My relationship with C. D. Wright was mostly about my trying to help keep the press alive after Frank's death. Everyone who was in that group of poets and artists has done good work in the world and I'm proud of them.

MM: What influence did the following people have on your work: Jim Whitehead, Bill Harrison, and Frank Stanford?

EG: Bill Harrison showed me the form of the short story. Jim Whitehead is one of my two best friends in the world. Frank showed me how to put a book together and how to believe in my instinctive sense of what a book should be.

MM: What effect has living in New Orleans had on your work? In what ways is New Orleans a southern city and in what ways is it not a southern city in your fiction?

EG: If I had been somewhere else when I began to work, I would have written different books. I was in New Orleans, so it was the setting of much of my early work. New Orleans is unique in every way. It is a port, which always changes a southern or northern city.

MM: Will you discuss the image of the southern belle in your fiction?

EG: I don't believe in southern belles, but the hoop skirts were fun, and I have worn them. The best part was trying to get to parties wearing them. They don't fit in cars.

MM: Would you comment on the class barriers in New Orleans? As an outsider, I have seen a very stratified and closed society. Even university professors participate in it in rather petty ways. Also, what did you like and hate most about living in New Orleans?

EG: I don't think people in New Orleans are different in that way from people in other cities. In small towns, everyone has to get along. The larger the city, the more fear, and the more fear, the more people stop liking and understanding each other. Snobbery is childish activity. Grown people have better things to do. I loved New Orleans and learned many things from living there. I love the food and the smells and the beauty of the people, and the live oak trees and the park and all the good and bad things. I never liked the [French] Quarter and thought it dangerous and filled with people being exploited in different ways, but I wish I was there right now, sitting by the levee at night, eating beignets, and thinking up poems with Frank or Ralph Adamo, or planning stories for *The Courier* with Don Lee Keith.

MM: What are you working on now?

EG: I took my 11-year-old granddaughter to a book fair and noticed that there wasn't much of interest for people her age. When I was 10 or 11, I read a lot of adult fiction, but there were books about people my age that pulled me in and engaged me. Now there isn't much for my granddaughter, so I am writing a series of novellas for 11- to 15-year-olds. The one I am currently working on is a mystery story featuring Ingersoll Manning IV. He is 14 years old, six foot, two inches tall, and a genius. He meets Tammili, Nora Jane Whittington's daughter, one of the twins. I sent Lydia, her sister, off to ballet camp, so Tammili and Ingersoll could solve the mystery and get to know each other.

Notes and References

Chapter One

1. *Falling through Space* (Boston: Little, Brown and Co., 1987), 152; hereafter cited in text as *FTS*.
2. *In the Land of Dreamy Dreams* (Boston: Little, Brown and Co., 1981), 71; hereafter cited in text as *DD*.
3. *Rhoda, A Life in Stories* (Boston: Little, Brown and Co., 1995), viii; hereafter cited in text as *R*.
4. *Net of Jewels* (Boston: Little, Brown and Co., 1992), 358; hereafter cited in text as *NJ*.
5. E-mail interview with Ginny Stanford, 1 August 1996; hereafter cited in text as GS Interview.
6. *Victory over Japan* (Boston: Little, Brown and Co., 1983), 207; hereafter cited in text as *VOJ*.
7. *The Age of Miracles* (Boston: Little, Brown and Co., 1995), 122; hereafter cited in text as *AM*.
8. Rhoda Faust, interview, 7 August 1996.
9. Ellen Gilchrist, letter to Rhoda Faust, postmarked 30 September 1981.
10. Don Lee Keith, interview, 10 August 1996; hereafter cited in text as DLK Interview.
11. Ralph Adamo, interview, 5 August 1996; hereafter cited in text as RA Interview.
12. See the interview with Ellen Gilchrist at the end of this volume; hereafter cited in text as Gilchrist Interview.
13. William Harrison, letter, 10 August 1996; hereafter cited in text as Harrison Letter.
14. Quoted in William J. Walsh, *Speak So I Shall Know Them: Interviews with Southern Writers* (Jefferson, N.C.: McFarland & Co., 1990), 283.

Chapter Two

1. Personal interview with Kay Bonetti, American Audio Prose Library, February 1986; hereafter cited in text as Bonetti Interview.
2. Quoted in Ellen Gilchrist, *The Land Surveyor's Daughter* (Fayetteville: Lost Roads Press, 1979), vii; hereafter cited in text as *LSD*.
3. *Riding Out the Tropical Depression* (New Orleans: Faust Publishing, 1986), 17; hereafter cited in text as *RO*.

4. *Anabasis* (Jackson: University Press of Mississippi, 1994), 5; hereafter cited in text as *An*.

Chapter Three

1. Jeanie Thompson and Anita Miller Garner, "The Miracle of Realism: The Bid for Self-Knowledge in the Fiction of Ellen Gilchrist," *Southern Quarterly* 22 (1983): 101; hereafter cited in text as Thompson.

2. Margaret Schramm, "Ellen Gilchrist," *Dictionary of Literary Biography* (Detroit: Gale Publishing, 1993), Vol. 130, 180.

3. J. Randal Woodland, *Louisiana Women Writers,* ed. D. Brown and B. Ewell (Baton Rouge: Louisiana State University Press, 1992), 196; hereafter cited in text as Brown.

4. Dean Flower, review of *Victory over Japan* in *The Hudson Review* 36–37, no. 2 (Summer 1985): 313.

5. Wendy Smith, *Publishers Weekly,* 2 March 1992, 46; hereafter cited in text as Smith.

6. *Drunk with Love* (Boston: Little, Brown and Co., 1986), ix; hereafter cited in text as *DWL*.

7. Margaret Jones Bosterli, "Ellen Gilchrist's Characters and the Southern Woman's Experience: Rhoda Manning's Double Bind and Anna Hand's Creativity," *New Orleans Review* 15, no. 1 (Spring 1988): 8; hereafter cited in text as Bosterli.

8. Wendy Lesser, "Home Movies," *New York Times Book Review,* 5 October 1986, 18.

9. *Light Can Be Both Wave and Particle* (Boston: Little, Brown and Co., 1989), 5; hereafter cited in text as *WP*.

10. Roy Hoffman, "Smart Enough for Their Own Good," *New York Times Book Review,* 22 October 1989, 13.

11. Robert Olen Butler, cover comments on *Rhoda, A Life in Stories*.

12. *The Courts of Love* (Boston: Little, Brown and Co., 1996), 4; hereafter cited in text as *CL*.

Chapter Four

1. *The Annunciation* (Boston: Little, Brown and Co., 1983), 3; hereafter cited in text as *A*.

2. Charles Stubblefield, review of *The Annunciation, Prairie Schooner* 58 (Summer 1984): 108.

3. Susan Larson, Review of *Net of Jewels, Times Picayune,* 12 April 1992, E6.

Chapter Five

1. *The Anna Papers* (Boston: Little, Brown and Co., 1988), 27; hereafter cited in text as *AP*.

2. *I Cannot Get You Close Enough* (Boston: Little, Brown and Co., 1990),vi; hereafter cited in text as *CE*.

3. Jane Taylor McDonnell, "Controlling the Past and the Future: Two-Headed Anna in Ellen Gilchrist's *The Anna Papers*," *Contributions to the Study of World Literature*, no. 46 (Westport, Conn.: Greenwood Press, 1992), 187; hereafter cited in text as McDonnell.

4. *Starcarbon* (Boston: Little, Brown and Co., 1994), 17; hereafter cited in text as *S*.

5. Mary A. McCay, review of *Starcarbon, Times Picayune,* 1 May 1994, E8.

Selected Bibliography

PRIMARY WORKS

Poetry

The Land Surveyor's Daughter. Fayetteville: Lost Roads Press, 1979.
Riding Out the Tropical Depression. New Orleans: Faust Publishing, 1986.

Short-Story Collections

The Age of Miracles. Boston: Little, Brown and Co., 1995.
The Courts of Love. Boston: Little Brown and Co., 1996.
Drunk with Love. Boston: Little, Brown and Co., 1986.
In the Land of Dreamy Dreams. Boston: Little, Brown and Co., 1981.
Light Can Be Both Wave and Particle. Boston: Little, Brown and Co., 1989.
Rhoda, A Life in Stories. Boston: Little, Brown and Co., 1995.
Victory over Japan. Boston: Little, Brown and Co., 1984.

Novels

Anabasis. Jackson: University Press of Mississippi, 1994.
The Anna Papers. Boston: Little, Brown and Co., 1988.
The Annunciation. Boston: Little, Brown and Co., 1983.
I Cannot Get You Close Enough. Boston: Little, Brown and Co., 1990.
Net of Jewels. Boston: Little, Brown and Co., 1992.
Starcarbon. Boston: Little, Brown and Co., 1994.

Journal

Falling through Space. Boston: Little, Brown and Co., 1987.

Articles

"Going Sane in New Orleans." *The Courier* 12, no. 27 (8–14 June 1976): 6–7.
"The Living Contract." *The Courier* 13, no. 40 (7–13 April 1977): 6–7.
"Our Asian Exiles." *The Courier* 13, no. 2 (13–19 January 1977): 4–6.

SECONDARY WORKS

Books and Parts of Books

Brown, Dorothy, and Barbara C. Ewell, eds. *Louisiana Women Writers*. Baton Rouge: Louisiana State University Press, 1992. A series of critical and bibliographical essays, this volume on Louisiana women writers links all the essays with the common themes of gender and place. Barbara Ewell's introductory essay is a clear assessment of what it has meant to be a woman writer in Louisiana over the past one hundred years; it helps put different types of social and political marginalization into context. The individual essay that includes an assessment of Ellen Gilchrist's uptown New Orleans characters shows how some women have been forced to the fringes of society and helps readers understand Gilchrist's particular sympathy for outsiders.

Castille, Philip, and William Osborne, eds. *Southern Literature in Transition*. Memphis: Memphis State University Press, 1983. This collection of 12 essays covers general themes and issues of southern literature and some specific authors. The general essays give readers a sense of the tensions within southern literature and of the development of the South's view of itself as a region and as a part of America. What it means to be a southerner, the stereotypes of the South and the southerner, and the ideals clung to in the face of insistent homogenization of culture, all help to focus issues of southernness, whether in a single author or in a time period. Although Gilchrist is not discussed, this book is very helpful background reading for understanding the particular culture conflicts that contemporary southern writers face.

Lawson, Lewis A. *Another Generation: Southern Fiction Since World War II*. Jackson: University Press of Mississippi, 1984. Although this collection of essays on Walker Percy, Flannery O'Connor, Richard Wright, Harriette Arnow, Mitchell F. Jayne, and William Styron does not give specific attention to Ellen Gilchrist, it does have a thoughtful and incisive background essay on twentieth-century southern fiction that is helpful for putting Gilchrist in a southern context.

Walsh, William J. *Speak So I Shall Know Thee: Interviews with Southern Writers*. Jefferson, N.C.: McFarland and Co., 1990. Containing 31 interviews with a variety of southern writers, this book includes pieces on James Whitehead and Miller Williams, both members of the Fayetteville, Arkansas, community. The interview with James Whitehead is particularly helpful to Gilchrist scholars because of his influence on her writing when she was at the University of Arkansas.

Weaks, Mary Louise, and Carolyn Perry, eds. *Southern Women's Writing, Colonial to Contemporary*. Gainesville: University Press of Florida, 1995. A collection of southern women's writing from pre–Civil War to the present, this book has excellent introductory sections to each period: "The Antebellum South," "The Civil War South," "The Postbellum South," "The Modern South," and "The Contemporary South." The Ellen Gilchrist story selected, "The Expansion of the Universe," seems to lack, the editors point out, an affinity with southern culture. In fact, it is a move to the South that causes the conflict within the story. A Rhoda Manning story,

"The Expansion of the Universe" first appeared in *Drunk with Love* and illustrates Rhoda's sense of displacement and alienation, a quality shared by many contemporary southern women.

Wilson, Charles Reagan, and William Ferris, eds. *Encyclopedia of Southern Culture*. Chapel Hill: University of North Carolina Press, 1989. A thorough study of southern life, past and present, this encyclopedia is an excellent background tool for those studying southern culture.

Young, Thomas D. *The Past in the Present: A Thematic Study of Modern Southern Fiction*. Baton Rouge: Louisiana State University Press, 1981. A critical study of the southern literature that looks to the traditions of the past to understand the writing of the southern renaissance, Young's book examines how the past reconstitutes itself in the texts of William Faulkner, Allen Tate, Robert Penn Warren, Eudora Welty, Flannery O'Connor, Walker Percy, and John Barth. Although the southern literary renaissance is, according to Young, most definitely over, the book helps readers understand the forces—aesthetic, economic, and political—that gave it its power. The book also helps readers to see how post-renaissance writers deal with that literary era, and how fiction such as Gilchrist's integrates a knowledge of the past with the present.

Articles

Bauer, Margaret D. "The Evoluton of Caddy: An Intertextual Reading of *The Sound and the Fury* and Ellen Gilchrist's *The Annunciation*." *Southern Literary Journal* 25, no. 1 (Fall 1992): 40–51. Comparing Caddy Compson and Amanda McCamey in terms of incest, the article looks at the relationships between Caddy and her brother, Quentin, and Amanda and her cousin, Guy. Both young women, Bauer concludes, are the victims of social hypocrisy, yet both retain a strong value system in the face of the dishonesty around them.

Bosterli, Margaret Jones. "Ellen Gilchrist's Characters and the Southern Woman's Experience: Rhoda Manning's Double Bind and Anna Hand's Creativity." *New Orleans Review* 15, no. 1 (Spring 1988): 7–9. Looking at southern women's experience through the characters of Rhoda Manning and Anna Hand, Bosterli evaluates how Gilchrist's characters take control of their lives despite the social constraints that say that girls and women must be helpless, dependent beings. Rhoda survives by challenging the male world, and Anna Hand does so by transcending that world in her art.

"Do You Think of Yourself as a Writer?" *Furman Studies* 34 (December 1988): 2–25. "The Woman as Writer and Reader" was the title of a symposium held at Furman University in March, 1988, as a part of the Emrys Foundation's six-week celebration of women in the arts. Ellen Gilchrist, Josephine Humphreys, Gloria Naylor, and Louise Shivers participated in a panel discussion on the topic of women writers, and the article is the result of that discussion.

Ellen Gilchrist. Contemporary Literary Criticism, vol. 48. Detroit: Gale Research Co., 1988: 149–65.

McCay, Mary A. "Ellen Gilchrist." *American Women Writers,* supplement. New York: Continuum Publishing Co., 1994, 161–63.

McDonnell, Jane Taylor. "Controlling the Past and the Future: Two-Headed Anna in Ellen Gilchrist's *The Anna Papers.*" In *The Anna Book: Searching for Anna in Literary History,* 187–93. Contributions to the Study of World Literature, vol. 46. Westport, Conn.: Greenwood Press, 1992. This article looks at how Gilchrist handles the issues of "fiction-making, fictionalizing, memory, storytelling, and gossip" through the character of Anna Hand, the dying writer. The questions of silence and speech coupled with the issues of women's voices and the issues of women's place in the social construct are all central to McDonnell's reading of *The Anna Papers.*

Schramm, Margaret K. *Ellen Gilchrist.* Dictionary of Literary Biography, vol. 130. Detroit: Gale Research Co., 1993, 178–87.

Smith, Wendy, "PW Interviews: Ellen Gilchrist." *Publishers Weekly,* 2 March 1992, 46–47. This pleasant interview with Ellen Gilchrist at her home in Fayetteville reveals the author's relationship with her characters and discusses her search for a way to allow individual characters and extended families a voice in her fiction.

Thompson, Jeanie, and Anita Miller Garner. "The Miracle of Realism: The Bid for Self-Knowledge in the Fiction of Ellen Gilchrist." *Southern Quarterly* 22, no.1 (Fall 1983): 101–14. Thompson and Garner examine Gilchrist's ability to enter the female psyche and create a female point of view in *In the Land of Dreamy Dreams* and *The Annunciation.* The coherence of this female voice is achieved in the stories by the characters at different stages of development and by Rhoda, who appears in four stories depicting different times in her life. In *The Annunciation,* the writers point out, Amanda becomes the central focus of the novel, and her experience challenges the stereotypes of what women should aspire to in the South.

Book Reviews

Brown, Georgia. "Look at Me! The Writer as Flasher." *Mother Jones,* December 1988, 46–47.

Carper, Leslie. "Deep South, Deep Roots." *The Women's Review of Books* 11, no. 9 (June 1985): 4–6.

Flower, Dean. Review of *Victory over Japan. Hudson Review* 36–37, no. 2 (Summer 1985): 313–14.

Fowler, Doreen. Review of *Victory over Japan. America,* 27 April 1985, 351.

Hoffman, Roy. "Smart Enough for Their Own Good." *New York Times Book Review,* 22 October 1989, 13.

Hughes-Hallet, Lucy. Review of *Starcarbon. The Sunday Times,* 17 July 1994, 7, 13.

Johnson, Greg. "Some Recent Herstories." *Georgia Review* 45, nos. 1 & 2 (Spring-Summer 1990): 278–88.

Larson, Susan. Review of *Net of Jewels. Time Picayune,* 12 April 1992, E6, 8.

Lesser, Wendy. "Home Movies." *New York Times Book Review,* 5 October 1986, 18.

Lowry, Beverly. "Redheaded Hellions in the Crepe Myrtle." *New York Times Book Review,* 28 September 1984, 18.

McCay, Mary A. Reviews of *New Stories from the South: The Year's Best, 1995* and *Rhoda: A Life in Stories. Times Picayune,* 19 November 1995, E6–7.

——————. Review of *Starcarbon. Times Picayune,* 1 May 1994, E8.

Stubblefield, Charles, Review of *The Annunciation. Prairie Schooner* 58 (Summer 1984): 108.

Taliaferro, Frances. Review of *The Annunciation. Harper's,* June 1983, 76.

Young, Tracy. "Off the Cuff: Ellen Gilchrist." *Vogue,* September 1986, 415-16.

Index

The Author

Mary A. McCay is chair of the English Department and professor of English at Loyola University New Orleans. She teaches American literature and women's studies and has published extensively on American women writers in both *The Feminist Companion to Literature in English,* Yale University Press, 1990, and in *American Women Writers,* vol. 5, Continuum Publishers, 1994. She published *Rachel Carson* with Twayne's United States Authors Series in 1993. She has also written several articles and reviews on Ellen Gilchrist.

The Editor

Frank Day is a professor of English and head of the English Department at Clemson University. He is the author of *Sir William Empson: An Annotated Bibliography* (1984) and *Arthur Koestler: A Guide to Research* (1985). He was a Fulbright lecturer in American literature in Romania (1980–1981) and in Bangladesh (1986–1987).

AOK - 9340